# Christian–Muslim Relations during the Crusades

# PAST IMPERFECT

**See further**
www.arc-humanities.org/our-series/pi

# Christian–Muslim Relations during the Crusades

**Alexander Mallett**

**British Library Cataloguing in Publication Data**
A catalogue record for this book is available from the British Library

© **2023, Arc Humanities Press, Leeds**

ISBN (print) 9781641890199
e-ISBN (PDF) 9781802701319
e-ISBN (EPUB) 9781802701326

**www.arc-humanities.org**
Printed and bound in the UK (by CPI Group [UK] Ltd), USA (by Bookmasters), and elsewhere using print-on-demand technology.

# Contents

# List of Illustrations

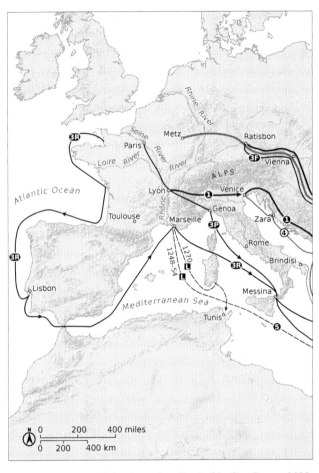

Map 1. Routes of the Crusades. Created by Ben Pease, 2022.

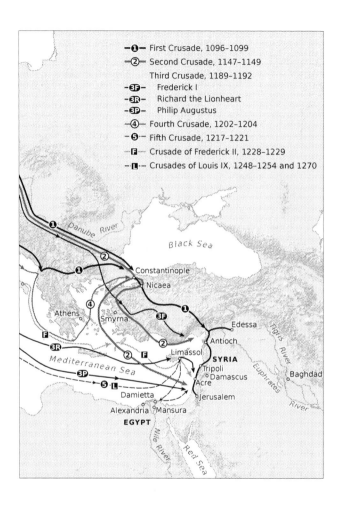

—❶— First Crusade, 1096–1099
—②— Second Crusade, 1147–1149
Third Crusade, 1189–1192
-❸F- Frederick I
-❸R- Richard the Lionheart
-❸P- Philip Augustus
—④— Fourth Crusade, 1202–1204
—❺— Fifth Crusade, 1217–1221
■F■ Crusade of Frederick II, 1228–1229
—■L■— Crusades of Louis IX, 1248–1254 and 1270

*Danube River*

Black Sea

Constantinople

Nicaea

Athens

Smyrna

④

❸F

❶

Edessa

*Tigris River*

Antioch

Limassol

**SYRIA**

*Mediterranean Sea*

②

F

Tripoli
Damascus

Baghdad

*Euphrates River*

❸R

❸P

❺ ■L■

Acre

Jerusalem

Damietta

Alexandria  Mansura

**EGYPT**

*Nile River*

*Red Sea*

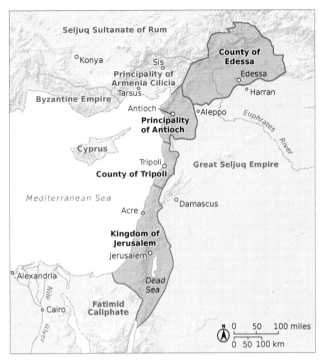

Map 2. The Crusader States at their greatest extent, mid-1130s. Created by Ben Pease, 2022.

Chapter 1

# Introduction

Of all the events of the medieval period, it is surely the Crusades which provoke the strongest reaction and continue to have the greatest political impact today. To some, they denote a sense of adventure and a noble quest or the actions of people motivated by sincere religious conviction, while to others they were a forerunner of the colonial period and the oppression of indigenous populations by western Europeans. What these viewpoints have in common, however, is that they view the Crusades primarily as a period of violence intensified by religious fervour, which both drove and resulted from the military conflict. However, a more careful examination of the two hundred years of the crusading period reveals that conflict was in fact rare. Battles were risky and armies were expensive. Instead, for most of the era a mutual accommodation was found between the various groups. This is rarely discussed in modern accounts of the Crusades, yet it is a crucial aspect of them for it demonstrates how, even in times of supposedly the most fervent religious conflict, people usually merely got on with their lives. The purpose of this book is to explore this underexamined aspect of the Crusades in order to demonstrate that they not only resulted in violent conflict, but also produced some of the most tolerant and multicultural spaces of the whole medieval period.

## The History of the Crusades

It was on November 27, 1095 that, according to traditional scholarship, it all began. A speech, one of the most significant and influential in history, outside the French town of Clermont was its catalyst. There, the Pope, Urban II, exhorted the people of Western ("Latin") Europe to leave their homes, travel to the Holy Land, and take control of the Christian holy sites, and particularly Jerusalem, from the Muslims. The effect was electric. Tens of thousands of people heeded the call and in 1096 joined the armies heading east under the banner of the Cross. These armies marched through the Christian Byzantine Empire and then Muslim lands in Anatolia, fighting off the Turks who tried to stop them. Having arrived in northern Syria, in October 1097 they besieged the great city of Antioch, which was notable as having been one of the four main centres of the Church and the place where the followers of Christ were first called Christians. After an eight-month siege the city was taken and, against all the odds, a huge Muslim relief army defeated. The first real test for the First Crusade had been passed.

The political landscape of northern Syria that the crusaders entered at the end of the eleventh century was extraordinarily complex. The region was full of small Muslim city-states, each ruled by a single Turkish commander whose power derived, in theory if not in practice, from the capital. It was the often bitter internal rivalries between the rulers of these cities that in no small part facilitated the First Crusade's victories at Antioch and other cities thereafter. Each cared primarily only about protecting their own position; hence Aleppo's ruler cared only for Aleppo, and Damascus's ruler only for Damascus. Despite the enormous size of the relief army that had been gathered in the failed effort to defeat them, Muslim attempts to counter the crusaders at Antioch were half-hearted at best. Indeed, after the city had been definitely lost some Muslim rulers in Syria even took to providing the crusaders with supplies as they marched south as a means of dissuading the invaders from attacking their own possessions.

Exacerbating these defensive problems on the Muslim side was the fact that much of the southern half of Syria, including Jerusalem, was ruled by the Fatimids, a Shii Berber/Arab dynasty based in Cairo that was intractably opposed to the Sunni Turks of northern Syria. In fact, the evidence suggests that they were more opposed to the Turks than they were to the crusaders, because during the siege of Antioch they sent an embassy to the latter suggesting that they join forces to remove the Turks from Syria and then divide control of the region between themselves. This offer was, however, rejected out of hand, and the crusading army reached its target of Jerusalem in June 1099. A siege of the town began immediately. After six weeks of desperate fighting, the crusaders stormed the city and, typical of the time, massacred a large part of the population. Many others, though, were permitted to leave. The crusaders then gave themselves over to both plunder and religious devotion. Soon after, on August 12, a Fatimid relief army from Egypt was defeated close to the city of Ascalon, near the coast of southern Palestine. Jerusalem was secured for Christendom and the First Crusade had achieved its primary objective.

Yet the situation was far from secure, as the Franks held only a couple of cities in a sea of hostile Muslim land. However, the geopolitics of the region worked in their favour so that, over the next two decades and with the help of a steady flow of reinforcements from Europe, the territory ruled by these Latin Europeans ("the Franks") gradually expanded. Cities were taken, one by one, from the Muslims—and, occasionally, from other Christians, such as the Armenians—all over Greater Syria (modern Syria, Lebanon, Jordan, Israel/Palestine) and in Anatolia. By 1124, almost every coastal city in the region was in their hands and four European-style states had been created, with their capitals in the cities of Jerusalem, Antioch, Tripoli, and Edessa (see Map 2, above).

The Muslim response to this Frankish expansion was negligible. This was partly because the rulers of what remained of Muslim Syria were both militarily and politically weak, and partly because they simply did not really care. The limited attempts they did make to counter the crusaders were primarily defensive, acting only when they themselves were threatened, and even then the few armies they sent against the Franks were almost all vanquished. Once in a while, one was able to defeat the Franks in a battle of local significance—particularly in northern Syria, as the armies of Muslim Aleppo and Frankish Antioch struggled for supremacy in the region—but in general the status quo reached by 1124 would remain for two decades.

Not until the mid-1140s was the first great counter-blow struck. In 1144, Zengi—an exceptionally violent Turkish warlord who ruled the two important cities of Aleppo and Mosul—took advantage of the absence of the Frankish ruler of Edessa to capture that city, with the majority of the surrounding county also falling to the Turks soon after. One of the four original crusader states was thus destroyed, less than fifty years after its foundation.

Subsequent Muslim propaganda would present Zengi's capture of Edessa as the culmination of his longstanding desire to fight the Franks, which, it was claimed, had been driven by the religious ideology of jihad. It was not. His attack on Edessa and its success was the result of luck and of taking advantage of the situation that presented itself, and the town was merely one of many in northern Syria that Zengi managed to bring under his control at the time, mostly from other Muslims. In reality, his rule showed little manifestation of jihad ideology or drive, and his death two years later aptly illustrates that, as he was murdered in his tent by one of his own slaves while in a drunken stupor. Hardly a shining example of how a jihad warrior should meet his end. It would not be until the latter part of the reign of Zengi's son, Nur al-Din (r. 1146–1174), that jihad would truly become a focal point of the Muslim struggle against the Franks.

Still, the loss of Edessa was a mighty blow to Christian Europe, and the shock reverberated around the continent. Almost immediately, plans were hatched for a new crusade to recover the city. This, the Second Crusade, was led by the German emperor, Conrad III, and the French king, Louis VII.

This marked the first time that individuals in such exalted positions had led a crusade, underlining both the seriousness with which the news had been received and the prestige that crusading had gained in the half-century since its inception. Yet despite having at its head such distinguished leaders and being much better organized than the First Crusade, the whole enterprise was an unmitigated disaster. After suffering enormous losses on their way through the Byzantine Empire—whose Greek Orthodox Christian ruler was at best unhelpful and at worst actively plotting against them—and, particularly, Anatolia, the armies entered the crusader states. Once there, they headed not for Edessa, in the north, whose loss had precipitated the expedition, but instead for Damascus, the largest city in southern Syria. Under its walls in 1148 the troops of France, Germany, and Jerusalem gathered, but their siege of the place ended in a total fiasco. They withdrew after only five days amidst a storm of mutual recrimination and bitterness. The abject failure of such a large and costly expedition dealt a heavy blow to the morale of the Franks and even left some in Europe wondering if crusading was a worthwhile venture at all.

Although in 1153 the Franks were able to take Ascalon, a coastal port in southern Syria that was the last town in Muslim hands, the mid-twelfth century marked the beginning of the long and inexorable decline of their power. In part, this was due to a gradual diminishing of material support from Europe following the costly failure of the Second Crusade. The development of various opposing factions amongst the nobility of the crusader states, and particularly the Kingdom of Jerusalem, also did not help. Yet the main cause was the gradual unification and strengthening of the Muslims opposing them. The main architect of this was Nur al-Din, ruler of Aleppo after the death of his father Zengi in 1146. Taking advantage of the fear that the Franks' siege of Damascus had caused within that city, in 1154 he seized control of it and the surrounding lands, in one move uniting all the Muslim lands of Syria under his leadership. For the first time, the Franks were faced with a unified Muslim opposition there.

Power, though, was still in the balance. Nur al-Din knew that he could not, at this stage, successfully attack the Frankish states. Not only were his forces not strong enough but, perhaps more importantly, the general Muslim population of Syria had not been psychologically primed for warfare. So began a concerted jihad propaganda campaign aimed at doing precisely that. Poems glorifying martial efforts were produced and read out, sermons exhorting the merits of jihad given, texts underlining the sacredness of both Jerusalem specifically and Syria more generally composed, and inscriptions highlighting Nur al-Din's jihad credentials carved into the new religious buildings whose construction he ordered. A central feature of this campaign was the construction of a great *minbar* (a pulpit for a mosque), ready to be placed in al-Aqsa mosque in Jerusalem in expectation of the future conquest of the city, once again, by Muslim armies.

Nur al-Din ruled Muslim Syria until his death in 1174. Yet it was not until the final years of his reign, a crucial period in the late 1160s and early 1170s, that his military struggle with the Franks began in earnest. By this point, the situation in Syria had reached stalemate, and so both sides looked around for an advantage that could help tip the balance in their favour. Both saw this in Egypt, where the Fatimid state, which had ruled that land for two hundred years, had become so weakened that an invasion looked particularly propitious. Adding to this was an internal power struggle between two rival viziers, each of whom was fighting to control the Fatimid caliph and, with him, the state itself. Thus, several times in the 1160s the armies of both the Franks and the Muslims of Syria invaded Egypt around the same time in support of one or other of the two candidates, hoping to see one sympathetic to their interests gain the vizierate and thereby secure for themselves access to the region's fabulous wealth. After some intense military activity, including a Frankish siege of the capital Cairo in 1168, Nur al-Din won out, and in 1169 his man took the position of vizier of Egypt. The Fatimid caliph was put to death not long afterwards and Egypt swiftly incorporated into Nur al-Din's ever-expanding Sunni realm.

The man who put an end to the Fatimid caliphate on Nur al-Din's behalf was the famous Saladin. Yet immediately upon doing so, he started to assert his independence in Egypt from his master and then, following Nur al-Din's death in 1174, slowly brought the lands of Muslim Syria under his own control in an act of brazen usurpation of the rights of Nur al-Din's young sons. In an attempt to legitimize his rather dubious rule, the spin doctors in Saladin's inner circle continued to produce the type of jihad propaganda that Nur al-Din had employed, and proclaimed that only he could defeat the Franks and recover Jerusalem for Islam. In no small part due to these efforts, Saladin's empire was soon consolidated and expanded even further. Within ten years of Nur al-Din's death, all of Muslim Syria and Egypt was under his control, and he was both the undisputed ruler of the region and the recognized head of the anti-Frankish struggle.

In contrast, over the same period the crusader states found themselves in the midst of an ever-worsening constitutional crisis, to the point where civil war seemed almost inevitable. Only the threat posed by Saladin forestalled this. Yet he could not be held off forever, and in 1187, having amassed an army consisting of troops from all across the Islamic world, he invaded the crusader states and defeated their forces at the critical Battle of Hattin, on July 4, destroying almost their entire defensive capability in the process. In the following weeks and months, he brought town after town, castle after castle under his control, recaptured Jerusalem for Islam, and almost put a complete end to Frankish Syria. Of the entire Kingdom of Jerusalem, the coastal city of Tyre alone remained in Christian hands.

The response of Latin Europe to the loss of the holiest city in Christendom was the Third Crusade, which was led by its three most powerful rulers: the German emperor, Frederick I Barbarossa; the French king, Philip Augustus; and the English king, Richard I. From each country, armies set out for the east, led by their respective ruler, as did troops from many other parts of Europe. The German army chose to go by the traditional land route via the Balkans and Byzantium

Figure 1: The Horns of Hattin, site of Saladin's famous victory over the Franks in 1187. Photo: Shutterstock/Ronny Hacham. Reproduced with permission.

into Anatolia. After months of successful marching, seeing off attacks in all three areas, in 1190 its leader, the emperor, drowned in a river just before reaching northern Syria, after which the army disintegrated.

In contrast, the French and English armies took the sea route east across the Mediterranean, arriving by ship at the city of Acre, which the small remaining force of the Kingdom of Jerusalem was besieging while it, in turn, was surrounded by Saladin's men. Over the next two years and despite Saladin's best efforts to resist, the crusading armies gradually expanded the area under their control, helped by regular arrivals of reinforcements from Europe. Eventually, with both sides exhausted and almost out of supplies, in 1192 a treaty was arranged that ended the almost five-year conflict. Neither side, however, was satisfied. The crusaders' attempt to retake Jerusalem had been in vain, while Saladin's forces had failed in their attempts to wholly remove the Franks from the eastern Mediterranean. Still, it was clear to both sides that the fighting could not continue. The French and English armies left for Europe, leaving behind enough troops and money to ensure the immediate security of the region, while Saladin sent his exhausted troops home. Less than a year later, he died.

With Saladin's death, the Muslim military struggle against the Franks also passed away. The empire he had constructed, stretching from the western deserts of Egypt through Syria to Mesopotamia, as well as south to Yemen, was divided up between the members of his family, the Ayyubids (r. 1193–1250). Though *de jure* approaching a family confederation with the ruler of Egypt as its head, it was *de facto* a series of rival and often hostile powers, each of which was concerned with either extending its borders or protecting them from outside incursions, depending on the relative level of power. Into the inevitable nexus of shifting alliances that resulted were drawn the crusader states, as well as the Christian kingdom of Armenia in northern Syria. The result was a delicate and somewhat harmonious balance of power across the eastern Mediterranean, a situation both produced and maintained by a series of treaties in which the crusader states often held a prominent position. Any attack on them by the Ayyubids would have upset this equilibrium and thereby threatened those Muslims' own positions while also, and particularly concerning for the latter, risking a new crusade being launched from Europe. The first half of the thirteenth century was, therefore, a period of peace compared to the final years of Saladin's reign. Both the Ayyubids and the Franks of the crusader states were content to criticize each other verbally in propagandistic outpourings, but there was relatively little in the way of direct military confrontation at this time.

Yet that is not to say there was none. The failure of the Third Crusade to recover Jerusalem was still keenly felt in Europe, and a number of crusades were launched in this period. The most infamous of these was the Fourth Crusade, which was diverted to and resulted in the capture and pillaging of Greek Orthodox Christian Constantinople by the Latin Christians of Western Europe. Some other comparatively small ventures were also organized against the Ayyubid states, such as the

Figure 2: The Saladin Citadel in Cairo. Photo: Shutterstock/Khaled ElAdawy. Reproduced with permission.

German Crusade of 1197 and the Baron's Crusade of 1239–1241, but these did little more than merely shore up the crusader states' fragile defences.

More significant than these were the Fifth Crusade (1217–1221), the Crusade of Emperor Frederick II Hohenstaufen (1229), and the first crusade of King Louis IX of France (1248–1254). The Fifth Crusade, which left Europe in 1217, was primarily called in response to the abject failure and embarrassment brought about by the events of the Fourth. Its aim was to regain Jerusalem by first capturing the Ayyubid's centre of power in Egypt. This would, it was reasoned, sufficiently weaken their ability to finance and maintain a defence of Jerusalem against the planned Frankish attack on the Holy City while also providing the Franks with the resources they would require in order to capture it. The Crusade took its first target, the Mediterranean port city of Damietta, in 1219 following a protracted siege of around eighteen months. After that, however, there was little movement for around two years, when the crusading army marched south in an attempt to take Cairo. This, however, proved to be a step too far. The crusaders were surrounded by the Egyptian army only a few days into their journey and forced to surrender Damietta. They made their way back to Europe in ignominy, having once more achieved nothing.

The Holy Roman Emperor, Frederick II, had promised to take part in the Fifth Crusade personally. However, he repeatedly delayed his departure due to domestic concerns until, eventually, the enraged Pope excommunicated him. In theological terms, this act de-Christianized the emperor and ensured he would not enter heaven when he died. Yet once he had solved his domestic problems, Frederick did lead a crusade to the east. Taking advantage of intra-Ayyubid conflict, the astute emperor struck a deal with the sultan of Egypt to give the latter military aid in an anticipated war with his rival, the sultan of Damascus. In return, Frederick would receive Jerusalem. Thus, in 1229, the Holy City was returned to Christendom via the diplomacy, rather than the military efforts, of the excommunicated emperor.

Jerusalem remained in Latin Christian hands until 1244. In that year, a nomadic group of Turkic Muslims known as the Khwarazmians entered Syria from the east, fleeing the bloody onslaught of the Mongol invasions. They, though, were hardly less aggressive, and attacked and captured Latin Jerusalem, slaughtering the population and desecrating the Christian holy places. The loss of the Holy City—forever, as it would turn out—once more galvanized Europe. In 1248 the French king, Louis IX, launched what would be his first crusade, once more against the Egyptian coastal city of Damietta. This time, the city's Muslim defenders took to flight upon the crusade's arrival there in 1249, and the place fell without a fight, in stark contrast to the events of three decades earlier. Once more employing the strategy of marching on Cairo in an attempt to seize Egypt before then trying to capture Jerusalem, the French army moved south along the Nile in November of the same year. The main Ayyubid army, though, was waiting for them and, in February 1250, they crushed the crusaders in battle and captured the French king. He was eventually released along with a number of other knights, but the vast majority of his army were either summarily executed or forced to convert to Islam. Louis' attempt to recapture Jerusalem was thus an abject failure, haunting him for years and eventually leading to his death at Tunis in 1270, on his second crusade.

The Ayyubid dynasty that ruled Egypt was overthrown in 1250, during and to a large degree as a result of Louis IX's crusade. Their own slave-soldiers, known as mamluks, rose up and killed the sultan, Turan Shah, before placing one of their own on the throne in Cairo. Thus began the Mamluk Sultanate, which would rule Egypt and Syria until the Ottoman conquest of 1517. Theirs was a militantly Sunni state, largely focused on purging the lands of all non-Sunni elements. Thus, over the next forty years, they slowly ground down and picked off the remaining crusader outposts in Syria, helped significantly by the considerable internal tensions amongst the Franks themselves. The last crusader city, the capital Acre, was taken and sacked in 1291. Those who survived the bloody massacre or enslavement set sail for Europe, where they delivered the news to a despairing though not particularly surprised audience.[1]

## Modern Scholarship on the Crusading Period

What may tentatively be called modern scholarly research into the Crusades began as far back as the seventeenth century. Often, the stimulus for this early work was to prove that

---

[1] There are many general histories of the Crusades available. Among the most recent are: Paul Cobb, *The Race for Paradise: An Islamic History of the Crusades* (Oxford: Oxford University Press, 2014); Niall Christie, *Muslims and Crusaders: Christianity's Wars in the Middle East, 1095-1382* (London: Routledge, 2014); Jonathan Phillips, *Holy Warriors: A Modern History of the Crusades* (London: The Bodley Head, 2009); Christopher Tyerman, *God's War* (London: Penguin, 2006); Jean Richard, *The Crusades, c. 1071-1291* (Cambridge: Cambridge University Press, 1999). See also the Further Reading at the end of this book.

Figure 3: Dome of al-Sultan al-Zahir Barquq Mosque, Cairo. Photo: Shutterstock/ Halit Sadik. Reproduced with permission.

one's own family had been on Crusade. The familial pride that was behind such efforts found its counterpart in national pride as countries such as France and England revelled in their crusading pasts, even as crusading—or at least its remembrance—continued in a somewhat altered form against the Ottomans who had invaded and were threatening much of Christian Europe in the early-modern period. As such, for centuries scholarship on the crusades focused almost exclusively on the exploits of the Latin Europeans, helped by widespread knowledge of Latin and other European languages among scholars as well as simply the greater availability of European source material. In contrast, knowledge and understanding of

Arabic and Islam were largely absent. In the earliest works, simply constructing a basic chronology and locating and editing relevant sources were overriding aims, while historical scholarship on the subject tended to proceed from a rather romantic perspective.

It was not until the late nineteenth century that more modern scholarly assessments started to be developed, as the field of history more widely became rather more "scientific" in approach. From that time onwards, scholars such as Carl Erdmann, Steven Runciman, and Joshua Prawer developed various grand theoretical frameworks that sought to explain the Crusades.[2] As is clear now, though, each of their ideas was profoundly influenced by either the societies in which they lived or their own personal biases. Erdmann, for example, saw in the Crusades a comparable historical moment to the militarization of Germany under the Nazis in the 1930s, through which he lived and had harshly criticized. Prawer, writing in the later 1960s and early 1970s—the period of decolonization—saw the Crusades as European proto-colonialism and thus also severely condemned them. In the 1950s, Runciman, in contrast, lambasted the behaviour of the crusaders primarily for personal reasons: they had attacked and destroyed much of his beloved Byzantium.

During the second half of the twentieth century, academic study of the Crusades took on a much broader focus than simply examining what had happened. For example, there has been much discussion among scholars about the seemingly simple question: "What was a Crusade?"[3] Other

---

**2** Carl Erdmann, *The Origin of the Idea of Crusading* (Princeton: Princeton University Press, 1978); S. Runciman, *The Crusades*, 3 vols. (Cambridge: Cambridge University Press, 1951–54); Joshua Prawer, *The Latin Kingdom of Jerusalem: European Colonialism in the Middle Ages* (London: Weidenfeld and Nicolson, 1972); Jonthan Riley-Smith, *The First Crusade and the Idea of Crusading* (Philadelphia: University of Pennsylvania Press, 1986).

**3** See the excellent discussion in Norman Housley, *Contesting the Crusades* (Malden: Blackwell, 2006), 1–23.

studies have sought to examine issues such as the nature of the institutions of the crusader states, of settlement patterns, and of the image of "the other" in writings from the period. Still more have focused on the evidence itself, either finding new sources, (re-)editing well-known texts, or translating them into modern languages, usually English.

As a modern academic subject, the Crusades straddles the usually very clear boundary between two traditional fields: medieval European history and Islamic history. As intimated above, scholarship has traditionally been focused almost exclusively on the Latin side, although this situation started to change from the very end of the twentieth century. While there were a few notable exceptions—the work of Claude Cahen and E. Sivan in particular[4]—it was only with the publication in 1999 of a seminal study of Islamic perspectives on the Crusades by Carole Hillenbrand that attention began to shift in that direction somewhat. Since then—and particularly since the attacks of 9/11—there has been, if not a flood, then at least a steady trickle of studies into aspects of the Muslim "side" of the Crusades.[5] Primarily, these have been focused on three main areas: political developments in the Muslim world; the theory, practice, and development of jihad during the crusading period; and the Arabic (and, occasionally, Persian) source material, much of which has been extremely neglected. However, the Muslim "side" of the Crusades continues to be comparatively under-researched, while attempts to fuse evidence and perspectives from both sides remain almost non-existent.

---

**4** Claude Cahen, *La Syrie du nord à l'époque des croisades et la principauté franc d'Antioche* (Paris: Presses de l'Ifpo, 1940); Emmanuel Sivan, *L'Islam et la croisade* (Paris: Librairie d'Amérique et d'Orient, 1968).

**5** See above, note 1.

## The Sources

In light of the importance of the subject for the history of Christian–Muslim relations, it is particularly unfortunate that research into the Crusades is hampered by the limited scope of the surviving source material. As is the case with much of the medieval period, and particularly before 1300, the vast majority of evidence comes from historical chronicles, works which provide chronological accounts of the events. Yet for all areas of medieval history, including the Crusades, these texts concentrate almost exclusively on the activities of the very top levels of society—kings and other rulers—as well as, in the case of Christian writers, aspects related to the ecclesiastical authorities and, in the case of Muslim historians, the most significant Islamic religious scholars. As a result, the activity and experiences of the rest of society—perhaps 99 percent of it—is generally, though not exclusively, passed over in the sources. As a result, modern scholars can but wonder about what came to pass in those areas of life that are not visible to modern eyes.

For some regions, such as Western Europe, this is partially compensated for by the fact that there is a plethora of surviving documentary evidence. This includes merchant records, charters and other legal documents, and parish records, which, taken together, permit a detailed reconstruction of life at all levels of society. Unfortunately, for the regions affected by the Crusades such evidence is almost non-existent. Due to the destruction that accompanied both the events themselves and subsequent bouts of violence in the Middle East—such as the Mongol invasions and Ottoman conquests—the majority of pre-Ottoman documents have been lost, and the few that remain provide only limited information on the Crusades.

Instead, the historian of the period fortunately has access to two other distinct yet complementary types of evidence that can help to reveal a broader picture of the societies of the Middle East at that time. The first of these is provided by two important and comparatively unusual pieces of surviving evidence. One is a travel narrative by the Spanish Muslim Ibn Jubayr who spent several weeks in the crusader states in the late twelfth century; the other is a book of personal anecdotes by a twelfth-century Syrian Muslim named Usama ibn Munqidh. These two texts contain a wealth of information about daily life in the crusader states in the twelfth century that is found nowhere else and, as such, can fill in, to some extent, some of the gaps left by the narrative sources. The second comes from sets of legal texts, such as those known as the Canons of the Council of Nablus, which was held in 1120. These contain lists of regulations governing relations between the different religious groups within the crusader states, and can be used to infer what was happening through the understanding that such laws were primarily promulgated in response to societal trends. Together, these two sets constitute important complementary evidence for interactions between Christians and Muslims during the crusading period, although it must also be remembered that both Ibn Jubayr's and Usama ibn Munqidh's texts are very limited in the type of interactions they report, while the laws are evidence only of what may have occurred rather than what certainly did. As such, modern knowledge of the societies of the Middle East in the twelfth and thirteenth centuries as a whole unfortunately remains very limited.

## The Scope of this Book

The aim of this book is to move away from traditional accounts of the events of the Crusades, on which much has already been written. In the main, and as may be inferred from the above, such studies have tended to focus on significant events or personalities, moving from one battle or siege to the next with occasional interspersing of deaths or diplomacy. While more recent explorations of the Crusades have started to move away from simply recounting the conflict between the two sides, instead adopting more thematic approaches, the conflict still looms large in the background; the Crusades, it is implied, were primarily a period of violence. This study will deliberately shift from that perspective. Instead, through an examination of the evidence for everyday encounters and relations between Christians and Muslims in five separate arenas, it will argue that the main result of the crusading movement was not, in fact, conflict but a socio-cultural situation that was as multicultural and tolerant as any in the medieval world.

Finally, a note on its limitations. The Crusades' geographical and temporal boundaries have been much discussed in modern research, with the result that many, though by no means all, scholars now view them in an extremely broad perspective. Geographically speaking, crusading occurred not only in the Holy Land but also in Greece, Malta, Spain and Portugal, Poland, Finland, and then into the wider world as the Spanish and Portuguese made their Voyages of Discovery. Temporally speaking, the Crusades have been seen as continuing from the medieval period into the modern, continuing right up to events of the eighteenth and nineteenth centuries as well as, by a small number of scholars, further back in time, before the traditional starting point of 1095. They were not even wholly—or, perhaps, mostly—aimed at Muslims. Instead, a whole range of actors could be on the receiving end of a Crusade, including Greek Orthodox Christians, groups of Latin Christians deemed heretical, pagans in parts of eastern Europe, and Jews. This study will, however, and primarily for reasons of space, focus mainly on what has traditionally been the core of Crusade Studies: those expeditions launched against Muslims living in the lands of the eastern Mediterranean and the years of Frankish settlement there (1095–1291).

Chapter 2

# Alliances and Treaties between Christians and Muslims

In October 1244, an enormous army assembled outside Damascus, the largest urban area in southern Syria. This force was composed of troops from both that Muslim city and from the Frankish Kingdom of Jerusalem, whose capital at the time was the coastal city of Acre. An eyewitness, the local Muslim preacher and writer Sibt Ibn al-Jawzi, provides the following description of what happened to members of the Muslim army:

> Crosses were above their heads and priests with the battalions were making the sign of the cross over the Muslims and offering them the sacrament. In their hand were chalices and drinking vessels from which they gave them to drink.... As for the [Muslim] lord of Homs...he began to weep, saying "I knew when we departed under the crosses of the Franks that we would not prosper."[1]

This combined Franco-Muslim army was the product of an alliance between the Ayyubids of Damascus and the Franks of Jerusalem in the face of a double threat to both of them: the Ayyubids of Egypt and the Khwarazmians, a group of nomads from the east who had fled westward in the face of the Mongol onslaught. The culmination of this episode was the battle of La Forbie (known in Arabic as Harbiyya), in which the Franco-Muslim alliance was crushed by the allied Egyptians and Khwarazmians.

---

[1] Hillenbrand, *Crusades*, 306.

Sibt Ibn al-Jawzi's words suggest the indignation that he felt at seeing the troops of his own city battle other Muslims alongside the detested, infidel, enemy Franks. Yet, as he would have known well as a historian, such a situation was hardly unprecedented, for Muslims and Franks had been forging strategic alliances with and fighting alongside each other ever since the arrival of the latter in the eastern Mediterranean in the late eleventh century. Indeed, such an alliance had been suggested by a group of Muslims as early as the siege of Antioch, during the First Crusade. In this case, according to the eyewitness Latin chronicler Raymond of Aguilers, an embassy from the Fatimid rulers of Egypt travelled to northern Syria and proposed to the Franks an alliance against the Turks, who had conquered the majority of formerly Fatimid lands in Syria in the second half of the eleventh century.

Although the Fatimid emissaries were sent packing from Antioch—primarily, it seems, because they had suggested that they, rather than the crusaders, should have possession of Jerusalem—it was not long after that the first alliances between Christians and Muslims were made. They were particularly prevalent in northern Syria in the first decades of the twelfth century, with two of the most noteworthy being those between the Franks of Edessa and the Muslims of Mosul on the one hand, and the Muslims of Aleppo and the Franks of Antioch on the other (see below). A few decades later, in the 1160s, the Franks of Jerusalem would form an alliance with one faction from among the Muslim rulers of Egypt in an ultimately fruitless attempt to prevent their mutual enemy, Nur al-Din, from expanding his sphere of influence into Africa. As these brief examples and the rest of this chapter will demonstrate, the alliance of 1244 was not, therefore, unusual.

## Alliances

As mentioned above, in the early years of the crusading period in particular numerous mutually advantageous alliances were forged between the Franks and the Turkish Muslim rulers of northern Syria. One such example, alluded to previously, comes from the year 1108, the result of a conflict between the two crusader states of Antioch and Edessa. The dispute had its origins in the immediate aftermath of the Battle of Harran, fought in northern Syria in 1104, when a Muslim force had inflicted the first significant military defeat on the Franks since their arrival in the area. In this encounter the ruler of Edessa, Baldwin II, and various other nobles had been captured. In order to safeguard Baldwin's city for Christendom, Tancred, the ruler of Antioch, became its regent and put one of his relatives in charge there. When Baldwin and his associates were released in 1108 Tancred and his relative were reluctant to relinquish their hold on Edessa, and so a brief conflict between the two sides was the almost inevitable result. In order to support their cause, Tancred and his followers allied with the nearby Muslim city of Aleppo, while the Edessans came to an agreement with Mosul. The resulting brief, low-level warfare was not a religious conflict between Christians and Muslims; rather, it was based on geography: the northern Syrians of Antioch and Aleppo against the cities of Mesopotamia, Edessa, and Mosul. This alliance neatly demonstrates how easily religious boundaries could become irrelevant for rulers on both sides if they believed it to be politically expedient.[2]

This saw perhaps its clearest manifestation several years later, in 1115. At this time, the sultan in Baghdad sent a large army to northern Syria in response to the pleas for help sent to him by Muslims of the region who had been displaced by the arrival of the Franks, led by the ruler of the Persian city of Hamadhan. Yet, arriving there, it found that the main Turkish rulers of the region had formed an alliance with Roger, the Frankish ruler of Antioch, against it because each Syrian ruler was greatly troubled by the approach of the vast army from the east. As a result of this agreement, the army of Damascus had set out for northern Syria to join those of Aleppo and Antioch, which had moved to confront the sultan's army. In the end, the latter was defeated in battle by the Franks

---

**2** Tyerman, *God's War*, 186–87.

of Antioch alone, but the situation is clear: a Muslim army sent to Syria from the east led to the creation of an alliance between the Christians and Muslims of the region against it.[3]

The situation was similar in southern Syria, where alliances between the Frankish capital Jerusalem and Muslim Damascus occurred several times in the first half of the twelfth century. One such example was concluded in 1140 in order to try to resist the growing power of "the most monstrous enemy of both kingdoms," as the Frankish chronicler William of Tyre put it.[4] This was the powerful Turkish ruler, Zengi, who, it was feared in both Damascus and Jerusalem, would soon pose an existential threat to both of them. This alliance between Christian and Muslim states was thus another act of self-defence against a potential attack by an outside force, a survival tactic used by both sides against a common enemy.

The forging of such outright alliances was only one manifestation of how positive relations between Christian and Muslim states played out during this period. More often though, this took the form of mutually beneficial treaties. One particularly instructive example of such an agreement was made in 1108, when, following a period of mutually destructive back-and-forth raiding across the borders of Jerusalem and Damascus, a four-year truce was agreed between the two sides. Not only did this put an end to the raids, but it also detailed how the crops produced by the regions of al-Sawad and Jabal Awf, in Transjordan between the two cities, were to be divided up between them: the Christians of Jerusalem would get a third, the Muslims of Damascus a third, and the local peasantry a third. Three years later the truce was renewed, with the Franks receiving half the produce of those lands, along with that of various other places. Over the next ten years, other areas between the two cities, such as the Biqa valley and Hisn al-Akrad (around the famous crusader castle of Krak des Che-

---

**3** Cobb, *Race for Paradise*, 120–22.

**4** William of Tyre, *A History of Deeds Done Beyond the Sea*, trans. Emily A. Babcock and August C. Krey (New York: Columbia University Press, 1943), 668.

valiers), had similar treaties applied to them. As the German scholar Michael Köhler has noted, by around 1120 such agreements covered the entire frontier region between Jerusalem and Damascus, from the Dead Sea in the south to the town of Homs in the north.[5] And agreements such as these would continue for decades after. To give just one example, the Muslim traveller Ibn Jubayr mentions one that was in force around the town of Banyas, between Damascus and Jerusalem, in 1184.[6]

Perhaps the most significant factor which lay behind such agreements was that Christian and, particularly, Muslim polities were often more hostile to each other than they were to their supposed religious opponents. Partly this was due to geopolitical considerations, as suggested by some of the examples above. Yet at other times it could, rather ironically, be religious reasons that drove certain groups to seek alliances across confessional boundaries. This is particularly the case with some Muslim groups, many of whom came from a variety of ethnic backgrounds and, crucially, different branches of the Islamic faith. Most of the Muslim rulers of Syria were Turks, and they followed the Sunni branch of Islam that had its religious and political centre in Baghdad. Yet the region was populated by a patchwork of other Muslim groups who were often opposed both doctrinally and politically to Sunni Islam and thus viewed as heretical by the dominant Turks. Perhaps the most famous of these were the Nizaris, better known in the West as the Assassins, who followed their own particular version of Shia Islam.

The existence of these intra-communal rivalries was a further major factor behind the establishment of cross-confessional treaties or alliances, and the weaker a group was, the more likely it was to seek one out. The Nizaris are a good case in point. They controlled a number of minor towns and castles across both Syria and Persia in the early twelfth century,

---

**5** Michael Köhler, *Alliances and Treaties between Frankish and Muslim Rulers in the Middle East* (Leiden: Brill, 2013), 87.

**6** Ibn Jubayr, *The Travels of Ibn Jubayr*, trans. Ronald J. C. Broadhurst (London: Cape, 1952), 315.

from where they attempted to spread their specific Islamic doctrine. However, they found themselves a major target for assault by the Turkish rulers of these regions not only because of their idiosyncratic religious views but also because they had the unfortunate habit of murdering their religious or political opponents in targeted killings. So, for example, Mawdud, the Turkish ruler of Mosul, was assassinated by the Nizaris in Damascus in 1113, and Aq Sunqur al-Bursuqi, the Turkish ruler of both Mosul and Aleppo, suffered the same fate in Mosul's mosque in 1126. As a result, in 1113 the Nizaris of Aleppo were massacred and they suffered the same fate in Damascus in 1129.

In consequence, at times the Nizaris came to arrangements with the Franks in attempts to protect themselves. For example, the Frankish chronicler William of Tyre reports that, in 1129 and as a result of the events in Damascus the previous year, they agreed to hand over to the Franks of Jerusalem the castle of Banyas, in the vicinity of Damascus, in exchange for an unspecified quantity of compensation. In 1149, the Franks and the Nizaris allied against Nur al-Din, even fighting and together suffering a crushing defeat that year to his forces at the Battle of Inab, in northern Syria.

It is important to underline here that it would be a mistake to label the Turks, who were the dominant players on the political landscape of the eastern Mediterranean in this period, as "local," or as any other term that would suggest that they were part of the native population. The Turks, Franks, and Nizaris had all only entered the region in the final thirty years of the eleventh century and they all ruled apart from most of the population. Most of the rulers of Syria also governed only one city. All this together meant that potentates of all sides had a rather precarious hold on their possessions and, as such, they habitually sought out potential allies wherever they could find them and made treaties whenever it suited.

The establishment of alliances and treaties between Franks and Muslims over the first half of the twelfth century merely continued the situation that had existed before the Crusades. In the final decades of the eleventh century, too, the

Turkish rulers of Syria, who had only recently gained control of individual city-states in the north of the region, often viewed with great concern the machinations of their overlords in Iraq and Persia. The latter could, in theory, remove them from their position at any time, and the Syrians had to guard against this. To that end, a regional alliance system was developed so that, should any threatening army arrive from the east, the local rulers would band together to resist it. The Turks continued to employ this system of mutual defence after the arrival of the Franks, who, being similarly threatened by Baghdad, as well as by Byzantium, simply slotted themselves into it, as the examples given above help to demonstrate.

The situation was rather different to the southwest of the crusader states in the same, early years of the crusading period. Here, the Fatimid caliphate of Egypt was the main opponent, and there are far fewer examples in the historical record of treaties or alliances between them and the Franks. Primarily, this was the result of a wholly different geopolitical situation from that of northern Syria, as the situation in the southwest had few of the factors that led to the large number of agreements seen in the north and east. In particular, the Fatimid caliphate was a comparatively strong, centralized state—unlike the fractured region of Syria—and did not face the threat of being crushed by another power as the Turkish-ruled polities did. Furthermore, a stream of almost uninterrupted Frankish military successes against the Fatimids between 1099 and 1124 meant that the former felt little need to come to any agreement during these early years.

The fall of the final Fatimid outpost of Ascalon to the Franks in 1153 marked the end of their presence in Syria, one which had, at a brief point a hundred years earlier, stretched as far east as Baghdad. It was from that high point that Fatimid power had gradually and inexorably begun to wane following the entry into the eastern Mediterranean first of the Turks, then of the Franks. With loss of territory came a concomitant loss of both financial and political power; this, in turn, led to internal divisions and serious weakness as they became restricted to Egypt. As noted in the introduction, as the power of both the crusader states and the Turks of Syria under Nur al-Din effectively cancelled each other out in the 1150s and 1160s, both began to look around for ways in which to secure or enhance their positions, and so the Franks started to explore the possibility of making an alliance with one faction among the Fatimids.

William of Tyre (d. ca. 1185), the greatest chronicler of the crusader states, provides an excellent description of an embassy sent from the Kingdom of Jerusalem to the Fatimid court in Cairo in the mid-1160s. The modern writer Stanley Lane-Poole produced the following dramatic summary of William's much more lengthy account:

> They were led by mysterious corridors and through guarded doors...they reached a spacious court, open to the sky, and surrounded by arcades resting on marble pillars; the panelled ceilings were carved and inlaid with gold and colours; the pavement was rich mosaic...here they saw marble fountains, birds of many notes and wonderous plumage, strangers to the western world; there, in a further hall, more exquisite even than the first, "a variety of animals such as the ingenious hand of the painter might depict, or the license of the poet invent, or the mind of the sleeper conjure up in visions of the night...." At last, after many turns and windings, they reached the throne room, where the multitude of the pages and their sumptuous dress proclaimed the splendour of their lord. Thrice did the wezir [vizier], ungirding his sword, prostrate himself to the ground, as though in humble supplication to his god; then, with a sudden rapid sweep, the heavy curtains broidered with gold and pearls were drawn aside, and on a golden throne, robed in more than regal state, the caliph sat revealed.[7]

This embassy was part of negotiations for an alliance between the two sides against Nur al-Din. The latter's forces had invaded Egypt in 1164 and consequently the Egyptian

---

[7] Stanley Lane-Poole, *A History of Egypt*, 4th ed. (London: Cass, 1968), 180.

vizier Shawar, desperate to cling on to his position, entered into these negotiations with the Franks. An alliance was agreed, and in the same year a joint Franco-Egyptian force trapped Nur al-Din's army near the town of Bilbays, not far from Cairo, forcing it to return to Syria. Several years later, in 1167, following another invasion of Egypt and a consequent siege of Cairo by Nur al-Din's forces, Shawar again allied with the Franks—in a supposedly perpetual peace—against the Muslims from Syria, who again were chased out of the country. As in northern Syria fifty years earlier, therefore, a comparatively weak Muslim ruler agreed an alliance with the Franks as part of an attempt to safeguard their own position in the face of a threat from some of their co-religionists from the east.

As noted in chapter one, following his death in 1193 Saladin's empire was split between his relatives. Although they were all part of the same confederacy, often referred to as the Ayyubid Empire and with the sultan in Cairo in the nominally senior position, there was in reality an often fierce rivalry between the different rulers. Each one sought to secure his own position against both predatory relatives and potential new crusades from Europe, both of which could prove fatal to his position. As such, they did what they could to prevent that from transpiring, including making alliances with or attempting to co-opt those Frankish forces that either did occasionally arrive from Europe or who were already present in the eastern Mediterranean, thus continuing in the first half of the thirteenth century the trend of alliances seen in the first half of the twelfth.

For example, even more so than the Franco-Damascene alliance of 1244 that was noted at the beginning of this chapter, perhaps the most famous instance occurred in 1229. In that year, the recently excommunicated Holy Roman Emperor, Frederick II, set out with a large army in an attempt to recapture Jerusalem. At that time, the city was under the control of the Ayyubid sultan of Egypt, al-Kamil. He was in conflict with his relative al-Adil, the ruler of Damascus, and believed that he could form an alliance with Frederick in order to use Frankish troops as part of his army in the predicted forthcoming war with his relative. In order to cement this alliance, al-Kamil agreed to cede Jerusalem back to the Franks, a move that at a stroke undid much of Saladin's work four decades earlier. Ultimately, the joint military alliance was not required because peace soon broke out between the two Ayyubids. However, the agreement between al-Kamil and Frederick had been made and so Jerusalem was handed over to the Franks without a single arrow being fired by either side. If we are to believe the contemporary Muslim writer Sibt Ibn al-Jawzi, in consequence "all hell broke loose in the lands of Islam," though to very little practical effect.[8]

The year 1229 was not the only time that an Ayyubid ruler offered to hand Jerusalem back to the Franks as part of treaty negotiations. For example, in both 1219 and 1221, in response to the Fifth Crusade's capture of Damietta, al-Kamil extraordinarily offered to hand back to the Franks almost all of the land that had formed the Kingdom of Jerusalem before Saladin's campaign of 1187. He also included in the offer the precious holy relic of the True Cross, which had been captured from the Franks at Hattin. This amounted to essentially everything that the Franks wanted, and more than they were eventually given in 1229. Almost unbelievably, however, they rejected his offer, a stance that has traditionally been blamed on the influence of the papal representative, Pelagius, who wanted the Crusade to capture Egypt as well as all of the Holy Land. Rather than embrace this unbelievable piece of luck, his attitude instead merely served to hasten the ignominious failure of that expedition. Precisely the same proposition was also made to the Franks around 1227 in return for their support in the intra-Ayyubid rivalries of the time. However, after these ceased the offer was altered to take the lesser form that was eventually accepted by Frederick. The 1229 treaty, therefore, marked the fourth time that Jerusalem had been offered to the Franks by the Ayyubid leader al-Kamil in exchange for either an alliance against a familial rival or

---

**8** Hillenbrand, *Crusades*, 221–22.

Figure 4: The top of the Church of the Holy Sepulchre, Jerusalem.
Photo: Shutterstock/MISHELLA. Reproduced with permission.

a peace treaty.[9] This steady flow of offers from this Ayyu-bid—who was, after all, a descendant of Saladin—to return Jerusalem to the Franks as part of treaty or alliance arrange-ments highlights not only how unimportant the holy city had become to that Muslim ruler—and how quickly—but also how closely linked to his political survival he viewed agreements with the Franks as being.

Away from Jerusalem, the Ayyubid period also saw the construction of alliances amongst the various polities of northern Syria. One such example comes from the first two decades of the thirteenth century, when one was agreed between the Franks of Antioch, whose ruler was Bohemond VI, and the Muslims of Aleppo, led by Saladin's son al-Malik al-Za-hir, against the Christian ruler of Armenia, King Leon II. With such agreements, the situation in the north in the early thir-teenth century very closely mirrored that of the early twelfth.

Treaties, too, were a consistent aspect of the political land-scape during Ayyubid rule. For example, the agreement made between Saladin and Richard I in 1192 that ended the Third Crusade was renewed in 1196 by Saladin's son al-Malik al-Aziz and Henry of Champagne, the titular ruler of Jerusalem. Other treaties were signed in 1198, 1204, and 1211. In the sources, a clear pattern can be discerned: usually the Franks waited for an existing truce to expire, made a minor attack on Ayyu-

---

**9** Phillips, *Holy Warriors*, 220–39.

bid lands, and then a new treaty would be agreed, most often to the advantage of the Franks. The Ayyubids themselves made few attacks on the Franks, mainly because they feared that the result would be a new crusade from Europe—whose states were growing more centralized and ever stronger—and which would, they feared, constitute an existential threat.

## Saladin and the Mamluks

Of all the leaders on both sides from the period of the Crusades, Saladin is the most famous, for it was he who organized the successful campaign against the Franks in 1187 that saw the army of the Kingdom of Jerusalem destroyed at the battle of Hattin and the city itself lost by Christendom. He also managed to resist the might of the armies of the Third Crusade, which consisted of huge numbers of troops from all over Europe, led by the kings of France and England. Yet despite this fame and success, his period of campaigning against the Franks was, in reality, fairly short. Only during a five-year period—from his invasion of the Kingdom of Jerusalem in mid-1187 until the signing in September 1192 of the Treaty of Jaffa which ended the Third Crusade—did he engage in combat against them. For a much longer period, between the death of his master Nur al-Din in 1174 and the submission of the city of Mosul in 1186, he campaigned against fellow Muslims.

This meant that, over the course of the years 1174 to 1187, Saladin's forces only rarely made direct attacks on Frankish territory. A much more regular occurrence were treaties with them, agreeing a truce. These were designed to prevent the Franks from interfering in Saladin's affairs, and particularly in his efforts to bring all of Syria, Egypt, and Mesopotamia under his control. William of Tyre reports that such were arranged between Saladin and the Franks in, for example, 1175, 1180, and 1185. Indeed, it was the very breaking of such an agreement by the Frankish lord Reynald of Châtillon in early 1187 that gave Saladin the handy excuse to launch his large-scale campaign against the Kingdom of Jerusalem later that year. Yet even during this period of campaigning, Saladin continued to make treaties with some of the Franks. He did not, he stated, want to attack the northern Principality of Antioch, nor the territory of Tripoli, whose ruler, Count Raymond, had accepted Saladin's overlordship for a brief period in the mid-1180s. As a result, both were for a time spared the attacks that devastated Jerusalem.

As mentioned in chapter one, in 1250, Saladin's successors in the Ayyubid dynasty were overthrown in Egypt by their own troops, slave-soldiers known as mamluks. Ten years later, in 1260, these slaves would also put an end to Ayyubid rule in Syria. Their uprising and overthrowing of the legitimate rulers—their own masters, no less—made the Mamluks usurpers and so required a considerable amount of justification. This they did by presenting themselves as the only force capable of resisting both the Mongol onslaught, which had devastated the lands of the Islamic east and would destroy Baghdad in 1258, and the Franks. They also proclaimed themselves to be the only group willing to enforce Sunni orthodoxy in the lands under their control, thus leading to bouts of intense persecution of the Jews, Christians, and Shia there over the course of their 250 years of rule.

Of all the threats at the time, it was the Mongols who were viewed as the most serious by the Mamluks because, having destroyed Baghdad and extinguished the Abbasid caliphate, they clearly had the capacity to pose an existential threat not just to the Mamluk sultanate but to the Islamic world more widely. As such, the Mamluks' energy was primarily directed at resisting them, while other opponents, the Franks included, were merely a nuisance. Yet because the Mamluks predicated their rule on a ruthless determination to carry out jihad against all enemies of Islam, the Franks were still a central focus of their military offensives. Thus, between 1260 and 1291 the Mamluks picked off all the remaining Frankish towns and fortresses in a concerted onslaught against them.

This was not, however, an uninterrupted offensive. Instead, on numerous occasions the Mamluks agreed treaties with the Franks, although these were made almost exclusively for political and military expediency at times when the Mamluks wished to launch a large-scale expedition against the Mongols, further to the east. Hence, what the Mamluks intended was to make short-term treaties with one or several of the Frankish states that would protect their lands from attack in one quarter or another while they focused their attention elsewhere. Examples of these were made with the Franks in 1267 and 1271. However, perhaps the most significant treaties made by the Mamluks during the late thirteenth century were a series involving the Mongol state known as the Golden Horde—based in southern Russia—the Byzantine Empire, and the Italian city-state of Genoa. This venture guaranteed the continued flow into the Mamluk state of its most important commodity: slaves from southern Russia, who formed the backbone of their armies. It is particularly significant in terms of crusading that it was Frankish Genoa that was profiting from this trade, in the process directly damaging their co-religionists in the eastern Mediterranean, despite the efforts of the papacy to stop such material aid being rendered to the Muslims.[10]

## Conclusion

Over the two hundred years of Frankish presence in the eastern Mediterranean, a broad pattern regarding treaties and alliances is evident. In the first half of the twelfth century, the many small and comparatively weak states of Syria, both Frankish and Muslim, attempted to create a balance of power within the region to ensure that no one of them could become too strong and dominant, either politically or militarily. Similar occurred during the Ayyubid period, in the first half of the thirteenth century, as each individual Ayyubid and Frankish ruler used a network of alliances or treaties, with people of both religions, in an attempt to secure their own comparatively weak positions. This was especially important in the case of the smaller polities, such as those centred on relatively unimportant Syrian towns such as Hama and Kerak,

---

**10** Phillips, *Holy Warriors*, 258–75.

whose tiny armies would have been no match for those of the bigger cities in a confrontation. The religion of their ally or treaty partner mattered little.

On the other hand, during the last years of Saladin's rule and the Mamluk period in particular, the Muslim states felt militarily and politically strong enough to embark on sustained campaigns against the crusader states. Yet even these times of intense military conflict were punctuated by treaties. The Mamluks, in particular, used agreements with the Franks during the second half of the thirteenth century in order to maximize their chances militarily against the much greater threat of the Mongols. Once that had been seen off, they either broke each treaty or waited for them to expire, and then gradually picked off the remaining Frankish strongholds one by one. These agreements were thus of an entirely different nature to those made during the early crusading period or under Ayyubid rule. Whereas in those periods, the treaties were made between two fairly equal powers, the Mamluks' overwhelming and obvious power advantage vis-à-vis the crusader states meant that during their period of rule they could dictate terms, and thus treaties that worked almost wholly to their benefit were signed.

Treaties such as these were not a new phenomenon in the political landscape of the eastern Mediterranean. Ever since the Arab conquests of the region in the seventh century, there had been a nexus of shifting alliances that, as often as not, crossed the Christian–Muslim religious divide. In the century preceding the First Crusade, for example, the Arab Muslim Mirdasid dynasty that ruled the city of Aleppo had placed itself under the protection of the Christian Byzantine Empire in 1030, while an informal agreement—a "non-aggression pact"—had existed between the Byzantines and the Fatimids. That the crusading Franks were almost immediately drawn into this pre-existing system that crossed the religious divide in the early twelfth century demonstrates how swiftly they both were accepted into the political landscape of the eastern Mediterranean by the Muslim rulers there and adjusted to the local political culture. This general state of affairs during the Crusades reflects wider trends across the medieval world. The main priority of rulers everywhere was to ensure their own survival, and making alliances and treaties was always a hard-nosed political choice. The religious classes could, and often did, denounce them, but the military leaders of society were more concerned with securing their positions than with any pious considerations. Thus, for a number of Middle Eastern states and their rulers, both Muslim and Christian, the Crusades and the Frankish presence provided opportunities for them to strengthen their own political position through alliances or treaties that crossed religious boundaries.

# Chapter 3

# Knowledge Exchange

Around the year 1000, Latin Europe was, generally speaking, a cultural, economic, and political backwater, with the glories of ancient Rome but a dimly recalled memory. The economy was stagnant and there was no centralized or centralizing state power strong enough to bring together the often warring petty states of the region. Consequently, there was little money or opportunity to keep the ancient knowledge alive, much less to create anything new. By the fourteenth and fifteenth centuries, however, this had all changed. By then, Latin Europe contained many strong, centralized states whose economies were booming despite the fighting that plagued the continent almost incessantly. The knowledge of the ancients, once almost lost, had been rediscovered and developed further. Philosophy, scientific enquiry, and medical knowledge became revivified, permitting further discoveries that would eventually lead to Europeans striking out from their homelands to discover the rest of the world.

It was the institution of crusading that was in large part responsible for this transformation in the continent's condition, for it was via the crusading arenas that the knowledge of antiquity, kept alive in the Islamic world and in Byzantium, passed into Latin Europe. The primary arena in which this occurred was the Iberian Peninsula, which was drawn into the crusading movement during the twelfth century as the Christian kingdoms of the north expanded southward and conquered territory from the Muslims during the *Recon-*

*quista.* Yet scientific exchange also occurred in Sicily and southern Italy—where the eleventh- and twelfth-century Norman kingdom and the thirteenth-century Hohenstaufen state contained significant numbers of Muslims, as well as Greek-speaking Greek Orthodox Christians—and in the eastern Mediterranean, where the crusader states provided Latin Christians with close contact with the central Islamic lands for the first time. In these three areas, Latin Europeans enriched themselves by rediscovering knowledge in a number of different fields, eventually leading to the creation of the modern world.

## Language Learning

The main mechanism by which all knowledge exchange between Christians and Muslims occurred was through the acquisition of at least one of the languages of the other religious group. Yet, as the rest of this chapter will demonstrate, the flow of knowledge was almost exclusively one-way, from the Islamic world to Europe. Consequently, language-learning was almost all one directional as well. While a significant number of the Franks learned Arabic, which was the language of science as well as of Islam, Muslims only very rarely seem to have learnt Latin, Old French, or any other Christian language. The only places across the whole Mediterranean that were exceptions to this were the Iberian Peninsula and Sicily, where large numbers of Muslims and Christians interacted, often on a daily basis, under Latin Christian rule.

From evidence in the Muslim sources, we know that many Frankish nobles who lived in the crusader states had learned Arabic. For example, Reynald of Sidon (d. 1202) is reported by the Muslim writer Baha al-Din Ibn Shaddad to have known both the Arabic language and Islamic history after employing a Muslim to teach him these, and he used his newly gained Arabic in negotiations with various Muslim rulers. Other important Franks known to have learnt the language included Humphrey IV of Toron (d. 1198), a Hospitaller scribe named Simon, and Baldwin of Ibelin (d. after 1267). It is also likely that the famous crusader Reynald of Châtillon learned at least some of the Arabic he knew during the sixteen years he spent as a prisoner in the dungeons of Aleppo between around 1160 and 1176.

Further evidence of this comes from at least three Arabic documents that were produced by the governmental apparatus of the crusader states. Two of these are now lost, but paraphrases were made by a Muslim writer in the fifteenth century, while the other is extant in the State Archives in Palermo (Sicily). Each of these documents was a type of contract, but their significance lies in the fact that they were written in Arabic, as it underlines that there was knowledge of that language and acceptance of its use in official documentation by some of the Frankish ruling classes. There is even minor evidence that some Franks knew the Turkic language spoken by the ruling Turks of the eastern Mediterranean, as suggested by a conversation recorded by the Latin chronicler Fulcher of Chartres between a Frankish knight and a Turk before the Battle of Hab in 1119.

As well as the higher levels of Frankish society, the scholarly outputs of various Franks also provide evidence of linguistic exchange involving Arabic. For example, the famous chronicler William of Tyre composed a now-lost history of the Muslim world entitled *Historia orientalium principum* ("The History of Eastern Rulers") based almost exclusively on Arabic-language sources. Other Latin writers, such as the Dominican friar William of Tripoli (d. after 1273), wrote various works that display their knowledge of Arabic, as well as of Islam, including one that William submitted to Pope Gregory X as part of an effort to increase missionary activity to Muslims. Others who knew Arabic and used it to translate texts into Latin include Stephen of Pisa (fl. early twelfth century) and Philip of Tripoli (fl. 1240; for further details of both, see below). As a final example, the late-thirteenth century friar Riccoldo da Montecroce travelled as far as Baghdad to learn Arabic, which he hoped to use in his attempts to convert Muslims to Christianity.

## Education

Perhaps the most long-lasting result of the discovery (or re-discovery) by the people of Latin Europe of scientific works through the acquisition of Arabic language skills during the crusading period came in the field of education. Their re-discovery, across the Mediterranean, of works on logic by Aristotle and other ancient authorities led to a move towards rationalistic argument and debate in European scholarly circles. Consequently, from the mid-twelfth century in particular, the study of God and of natural phenomena were to be increasingly influenced by logical arguments and approaches rather than merely accepting the ideas of the ancient authorities. This, in turn, led to a revolution in education in Europe, the founding of the first universities.

The earliest institutions that would be recognizable to the modern observer as universities in some sense had originated in the Islamic world, the initial one being established in the Moroccan city of Fes in the ninth century. Several centuries later, the first of these were founded in Europe, largely inspired by these institutions that had, by this time, been established in cities all across the Islamic world. A growing demand for more educational opportunities within Europe during the twelfth century eventually led to the foundation of these advanced new schools, outside the traditional monasteries and cathedrals, to which anyone could go who could afford to. Here, the teachers and students formed themselves into corporations (Latin: *universitas*) and lessons were focused on the ancient liberal arts, alongside other subjects such as medicine, law, and theology. They became so popular so quickly that, in 1179, the Church's Third Lateran Council was essentially forced to accept that education was no longer solely a matter for the Church, and secular education began officially in Europe. Among other things, this resulted in the foundation or official recognition of the soon-to-be world-leading universities at Bologna, Paris, Salamanca, and Oxford. In these cutting-edge institutions, knowledge derived from the Islamic world via Arabic texts was taught and, subsequently, improved upon within a number of different fields.

## Science

Throughout the entire crusading period, the city of Antioch, the capital of a principality of the same name in northern Syria, was a particular conduit for this transmission of knowledge from the Islamic World to Europe. One particularly active figure in this arena was Adelard of Bath. Having first learned Arabic in Spain and possibly Sicily, during his lifetime he translated from Arabic such important works as Euclid's *Elements*, the astronomical tables produced by the Muslim scholar al-Khwarizmi (d. ca. 850) and various sayings attributed to Ptolemy, many Arabic versions of which he obtained during time spent in Antioch. He also produced a Latin work on the astrolabe based on his study of various Arabic books on the subject. The ancient writers whose works he copied, he declared, used rational arguments rather than blindly following earlier authorities, and explicitly criticized his contemporaries in Europe for doing precisely the latter.

The work of Adelard and others in the early twelfth century was followed up in the later twelfth and thirteenth centuries, as the process of transmitting knowledge from the Islamic world to Europe continued. Individuals such as Leonardo of Pisa (the mathematician better known as Fibonacci), Theodore of Antioch, and Philip of Tripoli furnished Latin Europe with various scientific ideas through their links to Pisa. This Italian city-state was one of the main trading centres of the Mediterranean, from where the city's merchants crossed that sea, taking with them people in search of knowledge from the east. As the modern scholar Charles Burnett has highlighted, many Arabic–Islamic influences continue to be evident in Pisa, including in architectural forms, place-names, and family names, as is also the case in various other towns and cities across Europe.

Theoretical knowledge gleaned from Arabic texts in the fields of mathematics and astronomy, for example, was often accompanied and supplemented by that of a much more practical nature. This was particularly often seen in agriculture and especially in irrigation techniques, a case in point being the waterwheel. These had been a very common sight in the Middle East since before the rise of Islam, and even today some medieval examples survive, such as those in the Syrian town of Hama, which date from the twelfth century. The technology behind these wheels had been taken to Spain by the Arabs in the eighth century, where more were constructed to help improve agriculture in the dry south. During the crusading period, the people of Latin Europe came into contact with this technology in both Syria and Spain, and took it back to their homelands where it was used to help increase crop yields, thereby decreasing incidents of famine in Europe and allowing the population to increase significantly.

Another important piece of agricultural technology that made its way to Europe was the underground water channel known in Arabic as the *qanat*, used to irrigate fields of crops that could not otherwise get sufficient water. In the Muslim world they existed in places such as Egypt, where they were used to extend as far as possible the Nile's annual flood, and in the area of modern Iraq, where the waters of both the Tigris and Euphrates rivers were diverted onto the surrounding lands to increase their fertility and thus the crop yield. From around the period of the Crusades, this technology began to be used in Europe, too, and was so successful that it was subsequently exported by European powers, especially the Spanish, to their colonies around the world. Along with these new agricultural technologies came new crops whose production they helped enable, which, over the centuries, included rice, oranges, and lemons.

The Islamic world was not only an originator of technological innovations and goods that were taken to Europe during the crusading period; it was also a conduit through which those from other parts of the world reached the continent. One good example of this is silk, an item so important that it had a whole trade network named after it: the Silk Road. Silk originated in China and had been taken along the network that bore its name to India, Persia, and the Middle East for centuries. Although the product was not unknown in Europe before the Crusades, the presence of populations of Europeans in the Middle East led to a sharp increase in the quantity taken to Europe as part of a wider growth in trade between the two regions. Italian city-states in particular, who had gained trade concessions in many eastern Mediterranean ports following the First Crusade, brought large quantities of the luxurious material back to Europe. This, in turn, merely served to increase demand for it further. Eventually, the silk weavers of Italy managed to procure silkworms for themselves, again through trade networks involving the crusader states, which enabled them to both produce and process the material in their homeland.

Paper followed the same route. This, too, had originated in China before being taken slowly westwards into the Islamic world; according to legend, captured Chinese prisoners taught Muslims the art of paper production following the Battle of Talas, fought in Central Asia in 751. Over subsequent centuries, knowledge of paper-making slowly spread to the Middle East and then North Africa, before eventually arriving in Iberia, where places such as Xativa, in the southeast of the peninsula, became major manufacturing centres. From there, localized paper production slowly moved northwards into Christian Europe, to places such as Strasbourg and Basel. At the same time, the trade networks set up by the Italian city-states during the Crusades allowed paper to be shipped directly to Europe from the Middle East, where it slowly replaced parchment, the traditional medium for the written word in the medieval period.

## Medicine

Within scientific knowledge in general, the field of medicine in particular saw the (re-)introduction of knowledge into Latin Europe. This process had its beginnings a little before the crusading period, with the figure of Constantine the African (d. ca. 1090). He seems to have come from a Christian family in modern-day Tunisia and moved to Italy sometime in the second half of the eleventh century. Eventually, he became a monk in the famous monastery of Monte Cassino, where he translated various important medical works from Arabic into

Latin. As a consequence of his efforts, teaching of the subject in the universities of Latin Europe began in subsequent decades, and this was one of the key means by which the people of the continent were alerted to the knowledge that was written in Arabic and held in the Islamic world.

One particularly important Latin scholar who went to the crusader states in search of medical knowledge was Stephen of Pisa. Like Adelard of Bath, he travelled to crusader Antioch in the early twelfth century where he started to work on the Arabic text known as *Kitab al-malaki*, translating it into Latin with the title *Regalis dispositio* ("The Royal Arrangement"). This work, originally written in the tenth century and translated by Stephen in 1127, was a vast and extremely popular medical treatise consisting of ten theoretical and ten practical books, and it was one of the main bases on which medical knowledge was furthered in late medieval Europe. Stephen also translated Ptolemy's *Almagest* from Arabic into Latin. As with scientific works more broadly, the route between Antioch and Pisa that Stephen took would remain an especially central conduit by which medical works entered Europe from the Middle East for decades after. These included various Arabic medical texts by Averroes (Ibn Rushd) and sections of the anonymous but extremely influential *Sirr al-asrar* ("The Secret of Secrets"), which were translated into Latin by a Christian named Theodore—active in the first half of the thirteenth century—and circulated widely in Latin Europe. In other centres, such as Tripoli, translation work of medical texts was likewise carried out, as Philip of Tripoli, for example, rendered the whole of *Sirr al-asrar* into Latin. Arabic medical texts were also studied in Acre, the Frankish capital, by translation teams working in the thirteenth century.

The translation of medical texts from Arabic (as well as Greek) into Latin happened in all three of the areas of European contact with the Muslim world in the twelfth and thirteenth centuries and led to a wave of new knowledge in fields including surgery and pharmacology. Physicians such as Rolando of Parma, Gilbertus Anglicus, and Lanfranco of Milan all wrote surgical texts in Latin Europe during or immediately after the crusading period as a direct consequence of the knowledge obtained during that era. This, in turn, led to the establishment of new schools of medicine in cities such as Paris, Salerno, and Montpellier, where further developments in medical knowledge were made which would go on to have an impact all across Europe and the wider world.[1]

Precisely how these Arabic books came into the hands of the Franks is generally unclear. However, there is some evidence in the sources suggesting that at least some were taken in the aftermath of military victories. Whenever a Muslim army or caravan was defeated and its camp pillaged by the Frankish army, as happened fairly regularly towards the beginning of the crusading period at least, books were among the items taken. It is highly likely that medical treatises would have been of prime importance, not least because of the severe injuries suffered by many of the Frankish troops. A good example of this occurred in 1145, when the entire library of the Syrian man-of-letters Usama ibn Munqidh, comprising around four thousand volumes, was stolen from him during a Frankish attack on his caravan as he was moving from Egypt to Damascus. As Usama himself practised medicine during his life, it is almost certain that medical texts were among those taken. The medical knowledge contained within books such as these was then translated and taken back to Europe where it helped contribute to the major advances in scientific knowledge and to the development of new institutions.

## Geographical Knowledge

Before the twelfth century and the time of the Crusades, in Latin Europe knowledge of the world's geography had been extremely limited. Primarily, this was because many of the works of ancient geographical writers such as Ptolemy and Strabo were unavailable there, instead being kept alive in the

---

**1** Piers Mitchell, *Medicine in the Crusades: Warfare, Wounds, and the Medieval Surgeon* (Cambridge: Cambridge University Press, 2004), 206–11.

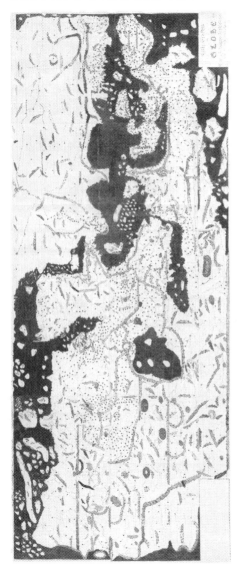

Figure 5: Map from the *Book of Roger*, by Muḥammad ibn Muḥammad al-Šarīf Abū 'Abd Allâh al-Idrīsī (1100?-1165?), general map of the globe taken from the geography of El-Edrisi, middle of the twelfth century, of the Vulgar Era. Paris, Bibliothèque nationale de France. Image in the public domain.

Byzantine Empire and the Islamic world. One of the very few works related to geography known in western Europe was the *Etymologies* by Isidore of Seville (d. 636). Furthermore, the region's economic stagnation, warfare, and political instability meant there was very little travel beyond its boundaries. With the exception of a few pilgrims to the Holy Land, the people of Latin Europe remained there. The twelfth- and thirteenth-century expansion of the European horizon, through the Crusades in particular, changed that completely.

One of the earliest examples of this new knowledge can be seen in the *Tabula Rogeriana* ("The Map of Roger," also often known as "The Book of Roger"). This formed part of an encyclopaedic work produced in Sicily in 1154 by a Muslim geographer named Muhammad al-Idrisi for the island's Norman ruler, and it contains some of the first detailed original descriptions of the world outside Latin Europe. Yet it was the presence of the Franks in the eastern Mediterranean for two centuries that led to knowledge of the lands both there and beyond being considerably improved. For example, the chronicle of the great twelfth-century Latin writer William of Tyre has the following report about Egypt, secured from some of the first Europeans who had actually visited:

> The whole territory of Egypt, from its furthermost frontiers, which are said to border on Ethiopia, lies between two sandy deserts which are doomed to perpetual sterility. Egypt would neither know nor produce fruitful harvests of any kind if it were not fertilized at certain times by the overflowing bounty of the Nile. The river, however, makes the adjoining areas fit for crops only if the lay of the land is suitable, for, where it finds a level surface near it, the river spreads out more freely and where it has spread out, it renders a wider stretch of land fertile. From Cairo downstream to the sea, the river finds a wide plain where it has free range. Here the fertile areas are thus spread out very freely and quite broadly. This both enriches the kingdom and also enlarges it....[2]

**2** James Brundage, *The Crusades: A Documentary History* (Milwaukee: Marquette University Press, 1962), 136–38.

It was in the thirteenth century especially that geographical knowledge of the wider world became much broader. This was a particular result of the missionary work within the Islamic world that had been started by Latin friars such as James of Vitry and St. Francis of Assisi during this period. They spent considerable time preaching in the eastern Mediterranean, in Egypt, and the Holy Land, and their example was copied by others during the later medieval period, who were to travel throughout Asia.

Primarily, this was performed by Christian monks of the Mendicant Orders, particularly the Dominicans and the Franciscans, who led lives of poverty as they moved from town to town preaching the gospel to the local populations. On the basis that crusading had failed to provide the victory for Christendom over the Islamic world that had been hoped for, and that various anti-Islam polemical works that had been composed had likewise failed, members of these orders were foremost amongst those who set out to preach to Muslims instead (for further details, see the following chapter), and some of them provided detailed descriptions of Asia. One of these was William of Rubruck, a Franciscan friar from Flanders who had been sent to convert the Mongols by the French king Louis IX. In his journey, which lasted from 1253 to 1255, he reached the main Mongol court at Qaraqorum (in modern Mongolia) where he engaged in religious debates with Jews, Muslims, and Buddhists. Returning to Europe, he wrote a long letter to Louis describing in detail the lands of Asia he encountered. Another who did so was the Florentine friar Riccoldo da Montecroce, who had joined the Dominicans in 1267. In 1288, he travelled to the eastern Mediterranean and stayed there for many years, returning to Italy around 1300. He wrote a number of works related to his travels, one of which was *Liber Peregrinationis* ("The Book of Pilgrimage"), in which he describes, in one of the first European books on the subject, the places and peoples of Syria, Iraq, and Persia. As such, during and as a result of the crusading period, the geographical horizon of Latin Europeans shifted from their homelands alone to instead reach almost as far as China.

## Magic

The translation efforts that led to the transfer of various aspects of knowledge from the Islamic world to Europe during this period was not limited to those fields that today would be labelled "science," such as medicine, mathematics, geography, and so on. Other knowledge, less "scientific" in the modern sense, also came into Europe, and particularly that related to astrology and magic. Works in these fields were translated by the same people who produced the Latin versions of scientific works because, in the medieval period, the line between "science" and "magic" was very thin, if non-existent. Magic, whether natural philosophy—a way of employing the underlying essence of the material world for one's own advantage—or sorcery—summoning up spirits to do one's bidding—required detailed knowledge of the often difficult pseudo-scientific theories behind them, in just the same way as medicine and mathematics did.[3] For example, during time spent in the Principality of Antioch in the first half of the twelfth century, the aforementioned Adelard of Bath obtained a copy of a work by the ninth-century Arab mathematician Thabit Ibn Qurra on casting talismans, which he translated into Latin. Others, such as Gerard of Cremona, John of Seville, and Hermann of Carinthia, did likewise, and their translations influenced occult beliefs in Europe for centuries thereafter. Thus, as in many other fields, the Crusades precipitated a flow of knowledge of the supposed principles behind magic from the Islamic world into western Europe, thereby providing Europeans with a store of information that would contribute towards many of the developments of European modernity over subsequent centuries.

---

**3** On this see, for example, Liana Saif, *The Arabic Influences on Early Modern Occult Philosophy* (Basingstoke: Palgrave, 2015), 9–94; and Charles Burnett, *Arabic into Latin in the Middle Ages: The Translators and their Intellectual and Social Contexts* (Farnham: Ashgate, 2009).

## From Europe to the Islamic World

Thus far, this chapter has focused exclusively on the movement of knowledge to Europe from the Islamic world because, during the Crusades, such movement was almost exclusively in that direction. However, there are occasional glimpses in the sources of knowledge passing the other way. Several of these concern Frankish doctors and their interactions with Muslim ones. The "memoirs" of the Syrian notable Usama b. Munqidh provide a trove of examples of this, which are, like much of his text, related in richly comic terms. As with almost everything he reports, Usama used these instances to demonstrate strange and wonderous occurrences in and aspects of the world. In the case of Frankish medical knowledge, Usama's view was clearly that it was strange because it was so backwards.

This can be seen in an anecdote in which a Frankish doctor gave a Muslim a cure for scrofula that was (to general amazement) found to be effective:

In Shayzar we had an artisan named Abu l-Fath, who had a boy whose neck was afflicted with scrofula. Every time a part of it would close, another part would open. This man happened to go to Antioch on business of his, accompanied by his son. A Frank noticed the boy and asked his father about him. Abu l-Fath replied, "This is my son." The Frank said to him, "Wilt thou swear by thy religion that if I prescribe to thee a medicine which will cure the boy, thou wilt charge nobody fees for prescribing it thyself? In that case, I shall prescribe to thee a medicine which will cure the boy." The man took the oath and the Frank said: "Take uncrushed leaves of glasswort, burn them, then soak the ashes in olive oil and sharp vinegar. Treat the scrofula with them until the spot on which it is growing is eaten up. Then take burnt lead, soak it in ghee butter, and treat him with it. That will cure him." The father treated the boy accordingly, and the boy was cured. The sores closed and the boy returned to his normal condition of health. I have myself treated with this medicine many who were afflicted with such disease, and the treatment was successful in removing the cause of the complaint.

That this Frankish remedy actually worked was clearly a cause of wonder for the narrator. Nevertheless, he duly noted its efficacy and thus provides some evidence showing that, on occasion, medical knowledge passed from the Europeans to the Muslims.

A particularly interesting perspective on this movement of knowledge can be seen in the changing Muslim understanding of the position of the Pope. In the first century of the crusading period there was scant, if any, understanding of it, little mention of the Pope in the Muslim sources, and no knowledge of the role he played in the crusading movement. However, a little over a century later, the chronicler Ibn al-Athir was able to say, in relation to the troops of the Fifth Crusade: "The organizer of them was the Pope of Rome, because he holds high status in the Franks' eyes. They hold that his orders should not be disobeyed nor his ordinances diverged whether in weal or in woe."[4] A century later the Muslim historian Ibn al-Furat was able to provide a comparatively detailed account of the role of the Pope in Latin society:

> Amongst the Franks the Pope is the caliph of the Messiah, in whose place he stands. He has the power to make things lawful and unlawful....It is he who crowns and establishes the kings, and, according to Frankish law, it is through him alone that they can be properly appointed.[5]

Yet perhaps the most significant field in which knowledge was passed to the Islamic World from Europe was in military technology. One of the prime factors that had allowed the Franks to be so successful in their battles with the Muslims was their clear superiority in certain aspects of this, especially naval technology. It was through their advanced ships and skill in navigating the Mediterranean that the Franks were able to

---

**4** Ibn al-Athir, *The Chronicle of Ibn al-Athir for the Crusading Period from al-Kâmil fī'l-ta'rīkh*, trans. D. S. Richards, 3 vols. (Aldershot: Ashgate, 2006–08), 3:174.

**5** Hillenbrand, *Crusades*, 320.

dominate those waters, allowing them almost uninhibited access to the Levantine port-towns while simultaneously denying the Muslims that same access. This, in turn, permitted them to reinforce the crusader states with troops and supplies without the Muslims being able to stop them, and to break any land siege that may have attempted. Similarly important was that Frankish field-tactics were often superior. The main offensive tactic, the heavy cavalry charge, could smash through almost any defence that the Muslims tried to set against it on the battlefield. The Franks were also much more skilled at making siege engines with which to try to capture towns and fortresses, not to mention that they had better access to supplies of wood for their construction.

Despite the often-seen derision of Frankish science in the Islamic sources, their advanced knowledge in military technology was clear to the Muslims, who attempted to emulate it. It is no coincidence that the two most successful opponents of the Franks, Saladin and the Mamluk sultan Baybars (r. 1260–1277), both constructed large fleets in an attempt to challenge Frankish maritime superiority. Furthermore, over the course of the period the Muslims learned from the Franks how to construct siege engines as advanced as any created by the latter, as well as developing methods to negate the heavy cavalry charge. In each of these cases, technology was passed to the Muslims by the Europeans, some of whom did so to profit, while others did so after converting to Islam. The Crusades were thus a means by which improved military technology made its way from Europe to the Islamic world.

Finally, over the course and as a result of the crusading period, knowledge of Europe's geography also increased in the Muslim world. Before the Crusades, what knowledge there was tended to be crudely stereotypical, rooted in the works of antiquity. For example, the tenth-century writer al-Masudi wrote:

> As regards the people of the northern quadrant, they are the ones for whom the sun is distant from the zenith, those who penetrate to the North, such as the Slavs, the Franks, and those nations that are their neighbors. The power of

the sun is weak among them because of their distance from it; cold and damp prevail in their regions, and snow and ice follow one another in endless succession.[6]

As a result of the Crusades much more detailed knowledge of Europe became available to Muslim writers. In texts from this period, the climate is described with much more accuracy, the geopolitical divisions are described in great detail—sometimes even at city-state level—political systems are sketched, and the policies of many of the European powers are explained. This was, to a large extent, the result of the increased diplomatic contacts that were in turn a natural consequence of the Crusades. One Muslim writer, Ibn Wasil, was himself a diplomat to southern Italy on behalf of the Mamluks and was thus able to give a detailed description of the political situation there as he found it in the mid-thirteenth century.

---

**6** Hillenbrand, *Crusades*, 270.

## Chapter 4

# Inter-Religious Knowledge and Perspectives

## Muslim Perspectives on Latin Europeans

Over the course of the nearly 200 years of the crusading period, Muslim writers produced many works describing the Christians from Europe. Most of these were less than flattering. They describe them as physically unclean, sexually promiscuous, having strange and exotic funeral practices, and (perhaps unsurprisingly) extremely belligerent. To these parochial (to the Muslims) practices was added the belief that they were religiously backwards, stubborn adherents to a religion that had been superseded by Islam. Of more direct concern, however, was that they were also religiously unclean, with the resultant belief among many of the more fundamentalist Muslims that the Franks' mere presence around Islamic sites was enough to pollute them spiritually.

These perspectives did not begin with the Crusades. Instead, they had their origins centuries earlier, and on two main bases. One of these were various Islamic texts, such as the Quran, hadith (the supposed sayings of Muhammad), and biographies (*sira*) of Muhammad, all of which contain sometimes strongly anti-Christian sentiments. These had originally been employed against the Greek Orthodox Byzantines but were taken and then applied to the Latin Christian Franks upon their appearance. The other consisted of primarily geographical works composed by ancient Greek authorities, such as Pliny and Strabo, which had been translated into Arabic and then incorporated into the Islamic worldview. In the latter,, a primary feature was the theory of the climes, which asserted that where a people lived in the world determined their appearance and behaviour. The Muslim world was in the third and fourth climes—the best ones—and so they viewed themselves as being the most attractive, cultured, sophisticated, and intelligent. The Latin Europeans, on the other hand, were in the fifth and sixth climes and so were stereotyped by Muslim writers as ugly, lazy, stupid, and backwards, in what was little more than a racist trope.

One such example can be seen in the following words by Said b. Ahmad, who was writing in the late eleventh century:

> Their [Europeans'] temperaments are therefore frigid, their humours raw, their bellies gross, their colour pale, their hair long and lank. Thus they lack keenness of understanding and clarity of intelligence and are overcome by ignorance and apathy, lack of discernment and stupidity.[1]

It was their Christianity, though, which meant the Franks were most often subject to the invective ridicule of Muslim writers. Insults such as "infidels," "polytheists," and "accursed" were regularly thrown at them, as were implicit accusations of idolatry, such as "worshippers of the Cross." This anti-Christian vitriol had its grounds in those aspects of the religion that are expressly refuted by Islam, highlighted in a mid-twelfth century description of the Franks from a Persian-language text called *The Sea of Precious Virtues*. One Christian belief criticized is the crucifixion:

> The most amazing thing is that the Christians say that Jesus is divine, that he is God, and then say that the Jews seized him and crucified him. How then can a God who cannot protect himself protect others?[2]

Another is the concept of the Incarnation, of God being born as a man:

---

1  Hillenbrand, *Crusades*, 270–71.

2  Hillenbrand, *Crusades*, 313.

> Anyone who believes that his God came out of a woman's privates is quite mad! He must not be spoken to, and he has neither intelligence, nor faith.[3]

The Franks' religion was, therefore, an object of ridicule for some writers, and continued to form the basis for many of the descriptions of the Franks. Yet perhaps the strongest theme is that of the religious pollution that they were believed to have caused. This was manifested in various ways during the crusading period, but certainly the most visually striking were the additions that the Franks made to the Dome of the Rock in Jerusalem, which was converted into a church. Here, the Franks secured a golden cross on the top of the building, placed altars inside, and added pictures and statues to the walls, all of which would have been anathema to the Muslims.

Some Muslim writers even suggested the Franks carried with them signs of spiritual pollution in their physical deformities. For example, Saladin's secretary al-Qadi al-Fadil described King Baldwin IV of Jerusalem (d. 1184) as "a blue-eyed, freckled, leprous evil-doer" in a passage that links his supposed physical deformities with his poor moral qualities. The Queen of Jerusalem, Agnes of Courtenay, Baldwin IV's mother, is called "the sow known as Queen who is the mother of the pig who is ruler of Acre" by Ibn Jubayr.[4] Since pigs are the primary unclean animal in Islamic law, this writer was demonstrating his contempt for the Franks for following a different religion by comparing them to those animals, although this explicit criticism masks a much deeper, implicit fear. Such presentations of the Franks—as essentially stupid people who followed an abhorrent religion and polluted the environment—are found in texts from throughout the crusading period. Their writers were extremists, but their opinions were readily taken up by other Muslims at the time and sub-

---

**3** Hillenbrand, *Crusades*, 313.

**4** Ibn Jubayr, *The Travels of Ibn Jubayr*, 316. Pigs are unclean animals in Islamic law, and Ibn Jubayr is here deliberately using highly offensive language.

sequently echoed down the centuries, so that they continue to influence some Muslim views of Westerners even today.

However, these were not the only perspectives, and some Muslim writers provided fairly neutral or even positive comments on some of the Frankish leaders, at least. Of the Holy Roman Emperor, Frederick II, for example, the thirteenth-century chronicler Ibn Wasil wrote:

> Amongst the kings of the Franks the Emperor was outstanding; a lover of wisdom, logic and medicine, inclining towards the Muslims because his place of origin and upbringing was the land of Sicily and he and his father and his grandfather were its kings and the majority of that island are Muslims... dialogues used to take place between the two of them [Frederick and the sultan of Egypt, al-Kamil] on diverse topics. In the course of that the Emperor sent al-Kamil complicated philosophical, geometrical and mathematical problems by which he might test the learned men he [al-Kamil] had with him.[5]

Ibn Wasil stayed in southern Italy in 1261 as part of a diplomatic mission sent by the rulers of Egypt to Manfred, who was the Holy Roman Emperor and Frederick II's son. His period in Italy seems to have left a profound impression on him, and his appreciation for the ruling household is clear not only in his comments on Frederick but also because, during this period, he wrote a book on logic which, highly unusually, he dedicated to the Christian ruler Manfred. Other Frankish rulers praised in similar terms by various Muslim writers include King Baldwin II of Jerusalem (d. 1132), Richard the Lionheart (d. 1199), and Louis IX of France (d. 1270). This comparatively restrained attitude was not, therefore, Ibn Wasil's alone.[6]

The reason for these varied descriptions of the Franks was the political situation at the time of composition. As noted in chapter one, the anti-Frankish effort saw peaks and troughs, and it is this that explains how the Franks and their actions are described. This effect can be seen most clearly in Muslim

---

**5** Hillenbrand, *Crusades*, 338–39.

**6** Hillenbrand, *Crusades*, 336–41.

writings that report the capture of Jerusalem at the climax of the First Crusade, in 1099. As likewise mentioned in the opening chapter, this resulted in the deaths of thousands of Muslims after the city was stormed. Muslim accounts written in subsequent centuries would bewail this in the most animated terms. Texts from close to the event itself, however, have a rather different perspective. The earliest of these was probably written in the 1130s, by al-Azimi (d. after 1161), a teacher and poet at the court of Aleppo. His description of the First Crusade's capture of Jerusalem reads simply: "[The Franks] moved on to Jerusalem and conquered it from the hands of the Egyptians, and Godfrey became its ruler. They set fire to the synagogue."[7] The next report was composed in the city of Damascus, close to Jerusalem itself, by the town chronicler Ibn al-Qalanisi around the year 1150 and is similarly brief:

> The Franks stormed the town and gained possession of it. A number of the townsfolk fled to the sanctuary [of David] and a great host were killed. The Jews assembled in the synagogue, and the Franks burned it over their heads. The sanctuary was surrendered to them on guarantee of safety.[8]

However, writing in the 1190s, almost a hundred years after the event, the Baghdad writer Ibn al-Jawzi expanded on this considerably:

> The Franks took Jerusalem on Friday 13 Shaban [5 July] and they killed more than 70,000 Muslims there. The Franks stripped the Dome of the Rock of more than forty silver lanterns, each of them weighing 3,600 dirhams, and a great silver lamp weighing forty Syrian pounds, as well as more than twenty gold ones and innumerable items of clothing and other things.[9]

---

**7** Alexander Mallett, "Al-'Aẓīmī's *Taʾrīkh* for the Crusading Period: The Years 489–508/1095–1115," in *Crusades* 19 (2020): 1–24, at 10.

**8** Ibn al-Qalanisi, *The Damascus Chronicle of the Crusades*, trans. Hamilton A. R. Gibb (London: Luzac, 1932), 48.

**9** Ibn Jawzi, quoted in Konrad Hirschler, "The Jerusalem Conquest

This is the most risible hyperbole. It is likely that the population of Jerusalem was only around twenty thousand, and even the arrival of villagers fleeing the Franks from the surrounding countryside would not have swelled the number inside to such an extent. There certainly was a massacre, but it seems to have been little worse than many others in the medieval period; the Muslim Turks had done exactly the same when they conquered Jerusalem thirty years before. The amount of goods described as taken is also wildly exaggerated.[10]

The clear difference between these two views of the Franks, neutral on the one hand and vehemently anti-Frankish on the other, was the result of the dynamics of internal Muslim politics at the time of composition. Anti-Frankish works such as those by Ibn al-Jawzi and al-Qadi al-Fadil were written at the height of the conflict, particularly the time of the Third Crusade, while the more neutral ones such as by Ibn al-Qalanisi and Ibn Wasil were produced in periods of relative peace. Consequently, the evidence reveals that the Muslim writers did not always hate the Franks. There were certainly some who did, although they were usually fanatics who despised anyone who was not a Sunni Muslim like themselves. With the exception of these authors, and of writings produced just before and during Saladin's reign as propaganda, Muslim writers were generally surprisingly neutral regarding the Franks or, in a few cases, even rather positive.

## Latin Perspectives on Muslims

The worldview of early medieval Christendom allowed for only three religious categories: Christians, Jews, and pagans (i.e., everyone else). This was the natural outgrowth of the "us against them" paradigm that had been widespread in

---

of 492/1099 in the Medieval Arabic Historiography of the Crusades: From Regional Plurality to Islamic Narrative," in *Crusades* 13 (2014): 37–76, at 55.

**10** Hirschler, "The Jerusalem Conquest," 50–51.

antiquity, and could be seen in the examples of the world split into groups such as the "Greeks and the Barbarians" and the "Jews and the Gentiles." It was the latter of these two from which arose Christians' own sense of self-identity; the Jews remained the Jews, the gentiles became identified with pagans, especially those of Rome, while the Christians became a third and elevated category of humanity.

However, with the emergence of Islam in the seventh century there arrived something that did not fit into any of these categories. Muslims were certainly not Jews or Christians, but neither were they pagans since they did not worship idols as the pagans of Rome and elsewhere did. This, though, presented Christian writers with a problem: How should this new religion be understood?

Initially, they took perhaps the easiest option and simply equated the Muslims with pagans and accused them, without foundation or knowledge, of idol-worship. While certainly inaccurate, it was justified with, on the surface, logical deductions. The Muslims were seen as having strange religious rites; they seemed to be deliberately targeting the Christians in the lands they attacked; and their rule had led to many Christians abandoning their faith. As such, in terms of the impact they had on Christendom, they seemed to follow closely the pagans of Rome. Crucially, however, equating them with those pagans was a means by which Christian writers could ensure that the readers understood their main specific point: Islam was, like Roman paganism had been, a threat to Christianity.

This presentation of the Muslims as pagans had begun almost from their very first appearance, but it originated not in works composed by Europeans but by the Christians of the Middle East, such as John of Damascus (d. ca. 750), who had been the first to encounter the followers of the new religion. Only after was it disseminated elsewhere, including throughout Latin Europe. As a result, writers such as Raguel (d. late tenth century) and Hrotsvitha of Gandersheim (d. 973) described in some detail the "pagan" ceremonials of the Muslims of Spain, in particular. However, this perspective started to gain even greater traction and to be placed front and centre around the time of the First Crusade, as the "fight against the pagans" became a rallying cry to recruit troops for the crusade and then to celebrate its victory.[11]

In one particularly memorable passage, the Latin writer Ralph of Caen (d. ca. 1120), who wrote an account of the First Crusade extolling the virtues of Tancred, one of its leaders, gives the following account of what happened when Tancred and his troops entered the main mosque in Jerusalem:

> A cast image, made from silver, sat on the highest throne. It was so heavy that six men with strong arms could barely lift it, and ten barely sufficed to carry it. When Tancred saw this he said, "alas, why is this image here which stands on high? What is the purpose of this image with its gems and gold? What is the purpose of this purple cloth?" For it was an image of Mohamet [Muhammad], entirely covered with gems, purple cloth and shining with gold. "Perhaps it is a statue of Mars or Apollo, for it could never be Christ. There are no insignia of Christ here, no cross, no crown, no key, no pierced side. Therefore, this is not Christ but rather the first antichrist, the depraved and pernicious Mohamet. If only his comrade were here, would that he came! For my foot would crush both of the antichrists here. Alas, alas, the fellowship of hell drinks in the Tower of the God and Pluto's slave is in the edifice of Solomon's God! Let this one fall quickly while that one also falls. Should he stand here arrogantly as if he had also conquered us?" The order was carried out immediately after it was given. The soldiers had never carried out any order as willingly as this one. The image was torn down, dragged out, torn apart and broken up. The material was precious metal but the form was vile. Therefore, something precious was taken from something vile.[12]

---

**11** John Tolan, *Saracens: Islam in the Medieval European Imagination* (New York: Columbia University Press, 2002), 105–34.

**12** Ralph of Caen, *The Gesta Tancredi of Ralph of Caen*, trans. Bernard S. Bachrach and David S. Bachrach (Burlington: Ashgate, 2005), 144.

This is, of course, nonsense. There were no idols, of anyone, in the mosque, and the author probably knew that. Yet he is presenting the scene in such a way so his audience would fully understand his view that: Islam was a degenerate religion whose followers worshipped idols; the First Crusade was a justified act; and, particularly important, it was the hero of his work, Tancred, who ultimately does God's work by destroying the idol.

Ralph was not the only Latin writer of the Crusades to present the Muslims as pagans. This perspective can also be found in the works of near-contemporary writers such as Peter Tudebode, Raymond of Aguilers, and Robert the Monk, and it is most evident in writings from the first decades of the crusading period, especially those recounting the First Crusade. However, after several decades and as a result of both the First Crusade and contacts elsewhere—in Spain and Sicily in particular—it had become clear to many that it did not reflect reality. Muslims were not pagans. As such, a number of churchmen became dissatisfied with it and so they began to formulate another perspective on Islam, one which, they believed, provided a more accurate understanding: that of Islam as a Christian heresy.

The basis of this was the revolution in knowledge brought about by the contacts with the Islamic World that were described in the preceding chapter. Through this, translations of Arabic texts were carried out in the crusader states and elsewhere from the early twelfth century. Among the most important were Quran translations commissioned by Peter the Venerable and carried out by Robert of Ketton in the 1140s, and by Mark of Toledo around the year 1210. Both were produced in Spain, and these were used alongside the Latin translations of Aristotle's works on logic to provide Quran commentaries for European audiences. These were, as may be imagined, fairly negative in nature, but they did give European audiences some of the first detailed and, in many cases, accurate insights into the Islamic faith.

Writers such as the French monk Guibert of Nogent (d. 1124) the German writer Embrico of Mainz (d. early twelfth century), and the abbot Peter of Cluny (d. 1156) were among the first to develop these. Their works are particularly focused on Muhammad, whom they present in similar terms to other famous heretical figures of late antiquity, such as Arius (d. 336), Nestorius (d. ca. 450), and, particularly, Mani (d. ca. 275), who were said to have used magic to pretend to work miracles and to have taken the true teachings of Christianity and changed them to suit their own nefarious ends. In these texts, the position of Muslims has been altered; they are no longer idol-worshippers, but instead a people duped by a false prophet into incorrect beliefs that would endanger their eternal souls.[13]

However distasteful such an assessment may be to modern sensibilities, it does at least have the advantage of being defensible from a logical perspective. While the idea of Muslims worshipping idols is patently absurd, Islam as a heresy is at least a plausible position to take from the perspective of medieval Christendom. For what is the difference between a heresy and a religion, other than its success or acceptability? From the medieval Christian perspective, Islam *was* a heresy, for Muhammad had, it was believed, taken Christian teachings and altered them in order to suit his own ends.

An important side-product of this new perspective, however, was a much deeper understanding of Islam in Latin Europe than had previously existed, largely as a result of the crusading movement. From this time onwards, Latin Christian writers knew many of the main aspects of Muhammad's life from the Islamic tradition (such as the supposed recognition of his prophethood by the monk Bahira and his marriage to Khadija), of Islamic practices (such as not eating pork), and of Muslim beliefs (such as that in one god and of Muhammad as a prophet).[14] Thus, contacts that were at least partially the result of the Crusades in the twelfth century led to a more accurate understanding of Islamic beliefs in Europe.

This continued into the thirteenth century, as Latin Christians started to focus on missionary efforts towards the Mus-

---

**13** Tolan, *Saracens*, 135–69.

**14** Tolan, *Saracens*.

lims. These targeted the realms of Islam and were pioneered by individuals such as James of Vitry—the bishop of Acre— and St. Francis of Assisi. They, in turn, helped inspire the creation of new religious orders, known as the mendicant orders, particularly the Franciscans and the Dominicans. Members of these orders, knowing that the earlier efforts to counter Islam through written polemics had failed, instead attempted to convert Muslims through preaching.

As their name suggests, the Franciscans were founded by St. Francis of Assisi, in 1209. A year later, they were officially recognized by the pope, Innocent III. One of their primary aims was to emulate Christ's apostles by wandering the lands, especially those governed by Muslims, preaching the Christian faith. They were devoted to poverty and relied on charity to survive as they made their journeys, following in the footsteps of their founder. In 1219, Francis travelled to Egypt on one of the vessels taking soldiers from Europe on the Fifth Crusade. One day, he moved from the crusaders' camp and travelled through the no-man's-land between the two armies, approaching the Muslim camp. Those he encountered thought he must have wanted to convert to Islam, but instead he asked to be taken to the sultan. There, in front of the whole court, he preached Christianity to the sultan of Egypt, at least half-hoping to be martyred for doing so. Instead, the sultan listened patiently to Francis before sending him on his way, back to the crusader camp.[15]

The Dominicans were also founded in the early thirteenth century by the Spanish priest Dominic de Guzman, and were recognized by Pope Honorius III in 1216. Their approach to preaching was founded on a scholarly, intellectual basis, and as such they attempted to prove the truth of the Christian faith to their opponents. Much of their effort was expended on the Iberian Peninsula and the areas of modern Morocco, Algeria, and Tunisia. However, some Dominicans were based in or travelled through the crusader states in the second

---

**15** John Tolan, *Saint Francis and the Sultan: The Curious History of a Christian-Muslim Encounter* (Oxford: Oxford University Press, 2009).

half of the thirteenth century. One of these was William of Tripoli, who was a friar at a Dominican monastery near the town of Tripoli, in modern Lebanon. He had studied Islam in great detail and, in a book entitled *Notitia de Machometo*, even gives a positive account of the religion. Another text he composed around the same time in the same place, entitled *De statu Saracenorum*, highlights in particular the great similarities between many of the core beliefs of Christianity and Islam. Another scholar who attempted this was Riccoldo da Montecroce, a Dominican from Florence. In 1290, just before the final dissolution of the crusader states in the Levant, he journeyed to Baghdad in order to learn Arabic so he would then be able to attempt to convert Muslims. Although he was successful in learning Arabic, his attempts at conversion were less so, and he returned to Italy around 1300, dejected, and devoted the rest of his life to composing anti-Islamic tracts.[16]

---

**16** Tolan, *Saracens*, 194–255.

Chapter 5

# Everyday Life

---

The Franks' conquest of a significant area of the eastern Mediterranean around the year 1100 brought, for almost the first time, large numbers of Muslims under Latin Christian control. In the immediate aftermath of these conquests by the First Crusade, Muslims living in the captured territory were subject to different treatment, which was usually dependent on how the area had been taken. In general, those towns captured by being stormed following a siege would be sacked and much of the population killed or enslaved. This happened at Antioch in 1098 and Jerusalem in 1099, for example. The alternative, and which seems to have occurred more or less equally frequently, was that places were captured after the population surrendered. In those circumstances, the people were usually given the option of moving away to Muslim territory or of continuing to live there under Frankish rule. This comparatively tolerant way of treating the populations of those cities captured by surrender contrasts with popular ideas about crusading, even though this was fairly standard practice in medieval warfare, in both the Middle East and Europe. There was nothing particularly noteworthy about this way of treating the inhabitants of the conquered regions.

It is impossible to make precise comments about the numbers of people who chose to leave their homes and move as refugees to lands still under Muslim control because evidence for this is almost wholly lacking. However, it is possible to trace some general patterns. From the chronicle evidence, it seems that, initially, a majority of Muslims chose to leave. Small numbers even travelled as far as Baghdad, where they publicly lamented the Frankish conquests and lambasted the Muslim rulers there for their failure to respond in any meaningful way. Most, however, merely moved to the nearest convenient Muslim settlement. For example, those who escaped from around Antioch moved a few dozen miles east to Aleppo, while those from near Jerusalem moved a similar distance to the area around Damascus, or to Egypt. However, many of those who did so were evidently disappointed with their lot, as help from their co-religionists was much less forthcoming than they may have been expecting. This was in sharp contrast to the Franks, who started offering generous tax conditions to those Muslims who would live and work in their newly conquered lands. As such, many decided to return home to their villages and live under the more favourable conditions the new rulers were offering.

Despite some attempts by members of the Latin Church to convert Muslims to Christianity (see Chapter 6), for the most part those who chose to live within the crusader states were simply left alone to get on with their lives, and allowed to practise their religion, for the most part, in peace. For the Frankish rulers, this made perfect sense. Had they brought a significant degree of pressure onto the Muslim population, the latter could simply have moved to nearby Muslim-controlled land. This would have deprived the Franks of the food and taxes that they produced, and which formed the economic backbone of the crusader states.[1] The system the Frankish rulers employed was thus mutually beneficial. Precisely who these Muslims were is, however, almost impossible to know. The lives of the ordinary people in the crusader states, as in virtually all parts of the medieval world, were not recorded by the educated elites of their society and so mostly remain unknown.

---

**I** This did happen, for example, with a group of Muslims from the region around Nablus who fled to Damascus in the 1160s following an intense bout of harassment from their Frankish overlord.

What has been observed by modern scholars is that most Muslims seem to have lived in villages in the rural areas of the crusader states rather than in large cities. Research into such settlements has highlighted that the majority were inhabited by members of only one religious community. As such, the Muslims who voluntarily returned to their lands in the new Frankish state centred on Antioch, in northern Syria, for example, generally lived in exclusively Muslim villages. Only the village head interacted with the Frankish ruler. This meant that there was very little contact between ordinary Muslims and their Frankish overlords,[2] and it is likely that, to the majority of Muslims living under Frankish rule, very little had changed.

A particularly detailed account of the situation comes from the late twelfth century. Writing of the situation in the Kingdom of Jerusalem in the 1180s, Ibn Jubayr relates how the Christians levied a small tax on the Muslims in their lands and that this gave the latter full protection. He ends his account by stating:

> [An] agreement exists between them [Franks and Muslims], and there is equal treatment in all cases. The soldiers engage themselves in war, while the people are at peace and the world goes to him who conquers....The state of these countries in this regard is truly more astonishing than our story can fully convey.[3]

---

**2** Ibn Jubayr mentions that, in 1184, he spent the night at a farm close to Acre that had a Muslim headman appointed by the Franks, who was in charge of the other Muslim workers; Ibn Jubayr, *The Travels of Ibn Jubayr*, 317.

**3** Ibn Jubayr, *The Travels of Ibn Jubayr*, 301. He expresses similar astonishment in his comments about the situation in Sicily, where the Muslim inhabitants of the island lived well under the Christian king: "Their king, William, is admirable for his just conduct and the use he makes of the industry of the Muslims....He has much confidence in Muslims, relying on them for his affairs, and the most important matters, even the supervisor of his kitchen being a Muslim; and he keeps a band of black Muslim slaves commanded by leisure chosen from amongst them." Ibn Jubayr, *The Travels of Ibn Jubayr*, 340.

On occasion, however, this arrangement did lead to problems for the Franks because Muslim villages sometimes rebelled if an army of their co-religionists invaded the region in which they lived. For example, the Frankish writer Walter the Chancellor, who wrote an account of the struggles between the Franks and Muslims in northern Syria in the 1110s, describes how Muslims who had been living peacefully in Christian-controlled land started making attacks on nearby Franks at the time a Muslim army invaded the region.[4] Another Muslim writer, Ibn al-Qalanisi, from Damascus in southern Syria, describes similar things happening around the same period near his city.[5]

Because incidents of violent resistance to the Franks, such as these, are among the very few times that Muslim villagers are mentioned in the source material, it would be easy to view them as the rule. However, they were, instead, the exception; they were recorded precisely because they were so unusual and, therefore, noteworthy. A more accurate assessment of the general situation comes once more from Ibn Jubayr, who relates his own experiences, from the year 1184, in his travel narrative:

> We moved from Tibnin—may God destroy it—at daybreak on Monday. Our way lay through continuous farms and ordered settlements, whose inhabitants were all Muslims, living comfortably with the Franks. God protect us from such temptation. They surrender half their crops to the Franks at harvest time, and pay as well a poll-tax of one *dinar* and five *qirat* for one person. Other than that, they are not interfered with, save for a light tax on the fruit of trees. Their houses and all their effects are left to their full possession....The Muslim community bewails the injustice of a landlord of its own faith, and applauds the conduct of its opponent and enemy, the Frankish landlord, and is accustomed to justice from him.[6]

---

**4** Alexander Mallett, *Popular Muslim Reactions to the Franks in the Levant* (Farnham: Ashgate, 2014), 51.

**5** Ibn al-Qalanisi, *Damascus Chronicle*, 101.

**6** Ibn Jubayr, *The Travels of Ibn Jubayr*, 316–17.

Ibn Jubayr's comments are particularly interesting because they reveal two contrasting contemporary Muslim perspectives on the situation. On the one hand, his own thoughts, clearly displayed, are those of an Islamic religious scholar whose primary concern was the spiritual wellbeing of members of the Muslim community. His perspective on good inter-communal relations was not positive. Instead, he viewed the situation as being part of a Frankish ruse to lure the Muslims away from their faith and towards Christianity. He comments: "Their [the Muslims living in Frankish lands] hearts have been seduced, for they observe how unlike them in ease and comfort are their brethren in the Muslim regions under their [Muslim] governors. This is one of the misfortunes afflicting the Muslims";[7] and a little later, at the height of his vitriol, he declares that "there can be no excuse in the eyes of God for a Muslim to stay in any infidel country."[8] From his perspective this could lead to their seduction and so the potential danger of dragging them to Hell, as well as of allowing further Muslim territory to be lost to the Christians.

In contrast, and in opposition to his spiritual concerns, the Muslim peasants whom he describes would likely have had very different, more material concerns, such as day-to-day survival, justice, and fair treatment from their master. It is thus unsurprising many of them would have been happy living under one who was of a different religion, as long as such conditions were met. Thus, in Ibn Jubayr's work, it is possible to see the ambiguous feelings that prolonged contact with the Franks produced in the Muslim community. Having seen the comparatively good treatment of these Muslims by their Christian rulers, Ibn Jubayr was exposed to a reality he did not want to, or could not, fully accept. From his eyewitness experience, the Latin Christians, described in Muslim propaganda at the time as followers of Satan, polluters of Islamic lands, worthy of death, and so on, were not, on the surface at least, the monsters he would have imagined. Yet so deeply

---

**7** Ibn Jubayr, *The Travels of Ibn Jubayr*.

**8** Ibn Jubayr, *The Travels of Ibn Jubayr*, 321.

ingrained was the "official" religious propaganda against them that he had to ascribe deliberately devious motives to the Franks' good treatment of the Muslims who lived in the villages.

As well as those who dwelt in the countryside, there is some evidence that a few Muslims at least lived in Frankish towns and cities as well, at least in the early crusading period. Reporting the testimony of some Muslims he met in Frankish Tyre in 1184, Ibn Jubayr relates that, after the conquest of the place sixty years earlier, the Muslims who had been living there had departed for Islamic territory elsewhere. However, finding that they missed their hometown too much, some of them decided to return to it to live under the Franks, who allowed them to keep a mosque there.

Despite this, however, it should not be presumed that people lived alongside each other in multicultural and multi-ethnic urban settlements. There were large cities where people from all religious backgrounds could live together, such as Jerusalem, Acre, and Antioch, but these were the exception rather than the rule. And, for the most part, the extent to which the Muslims living in Frankish towns and cities can be regarded as permanent residents is also debatable. Indeed, the modern scholar Jacoby has gone so far as to suggest that there were no permanent Muslim residents in thirteenth-century Acre, although he also admits that some did reside there for many years as traders. For those who did, there is no evidence that any constraints were put in place for the Muslim inhabitants beyond the taxes they had to pay. In contrast, Christian merchants—who were primarily from the Italian trading city-states of Venice, Pisa, and Genoa—faced much greater constraints, such as restrictions on their movements, when staying in Muslim trading centres such as Alexandria.

The ordinary Muslims who found themselves living in lands conquered by the Franks seem, therefore, to have had a relatively comfortable existence for the time. Ibn Jubayr's comment, noted above—that "the Muslim community bewails the injustice of a landlord of its own faith, and applauds the conduct of its opponent and enemy, the Frankish landlord, and is accustomed to justice from him"—even suggests that their lives were actually better under the Franks than under Muslim rule. Here, a stark contrast can be drawn with the situation later in the crusading period when Muslims re-conquered lands from the Franks. At that time, the Franks were usually given the same conditions as they had given Muslims; if the town was captured by force, they would be killed or enslaved, while if the town was surrendered they would usually be allowed to leave. However, they were not generally allowed to live under Muslim rule as Latin Christians; if they wanted to remain where they were then they would have had to convert to Islam. Only Native Christians, who had lived in the area for centuries, were permitted to remain Christian under re-established Islamic rule.

## Professional Exchanges

As highlighted above, significant numbers of Muslims lived under Frankish rule and worked the land for them, producing food and taxes. From Ibn Jubayr's evidence, the village headman, at least, would have had dealings with the Franks in what may broadly be termed a professional capacity when giving them the taxes produced by his village. This was just one of a variety of ways in which Franks and Muslims encountered each other in their professional lives. Another common route was trade. Ibn Jubayr again reports the following, from the late twelfth century:

> One of the astonishing things that is talked of is that though the fires of discord burn between the two parties, Muslim and Christian, two armies of them may meet and dispose themselves in battle array, and yet Muslim and Christian travelers will come and go between them without interference...[as an example, while Saladin was closely besieging the Frankish fortress of Kerak] still the [Muslim] caravans passed successively from Egypt to Damascus, going through the lands of the Franks without impediment from them. In the same way the Muslims continuously journeyed from Damascus to Acre (in Frankish territory), and likewise

not one of the Christian merchants was stopped or hindered
(in Muslim territories).[9]

The existence of mutually hostile armies thus does not
appear to have had a significant impact on trade between
the two sides. Indeed, the fighting between them could even
lead to new opportunities, as merchants often followed their
armies, selling things to the troops. For example, following
the cessation of hostilities between Saladin and the Franks
in 1192, a group of Muslim merchants who had been following the sultan's army immediately went to Jaffa to trade with
the Franks there.[10] Likewise, during the time of the siege of
Damietta by the Fifth Crusade, around the year 1220, there
is evidence that people from the local population of Egypt
took advantage of the presence of this army by selling crops
and, in some cases, going fishing in the Mediterranean and
then selling their catches to the Frankish troops.[11] The Muslim merchants of Damascus sold weapons to the Franks just
before the battle of La Forbie in 1244, and there was a large
hostel (*funduq*) for Muslim merchants in Frankish Acre in the
years before the Mamluk conquest of the city in 1291. Indeed,
it was the murder of two Muslim merchants in that city that
formed the pretext for the final assault on it by the Mamluks
that year.[12]

As well as trade, professional exchanges occurred in the
realm of medical knowledge, as noted in general terms in
Chapter 3 regarding how knowledge moved from one society
to another. Further evidence exists regarding how Frankish and
Muslim doctors from both sides worked together or interacted
personally in a professional capacity, thereby continuing a

---

**9** Ibn Jubayr, *The Travels of Ibn Jubayr*, 300–1.

**10** Al-Maqrizi, *A History of the Ayyubid Sultans of Egypt*, trans. Ronald
J. C. Broadhurst (Boston: Twayne, 1980), 97.

**11** *History of the Patriarchs of the Egyptian Church*, ed. and trans.
Aziz Atiya et al., 4 vols. with multiple parts (Cairo: n.p., 1943–74),
3, pt. 2:219.

**12** Mallett, *Popular Muslim Reactions*, 136.

trend involving Christian and Muslim physicians that had gone on for centuries previously in the Islamic world. One example was reported to Usama ibn Munqidh by a local physician:

> They [the Franks] brought before me a knight in whose leg an abscess had grown; and a woman afflicted with imbecility. To the knight I applied a small poultice until the abscess opened and became well; and the woman I put on a diet and made her humor wet. Then a Frankish physician came to them and said, "This man knows nothing about treating them." He then said to the knight, "Which wouldst thou prefer, living with one leg or dying with two?" The latter replied, "Living with one leg." The physician said, "Bring me a strong knight and a sharp ax." A knight came with the ax. And I was standing by. Then the physician laid the leg of the patient on a block of wood and bade the knight strike his leg with the ax and chop it off at one blow. Accordingly he struck it – while I was looking on – one blow, but the leg was not severed. He dealt another blow, upon which the marrow of the leg flowed out and the patient died on the spot. He then examined the woman and said, "This is a woman in whose head there is a devil which has possessed her. Shave off her hair." Accordingly they shaved it off and the woman began once more to eat their ordinary diet – garlic and mustard. Her imbecility took a turn for the worse. The physician then said, "The devil has penetrated her head." He therefore took a razor, made a deep cruciform incision on it, peeled off the skin at the middle of the incision until the bone of the skull was exposed and rubbed it with salt. The woman also expired immediately. Thereupon I asked them whether my services were needed any longer, and when they replied in the negative I returned home, having learned of their medicine what I knew not before.[13]

Despite clearly playing on the prejudices of his Muslim readers regarding both the inferiority and absurdity of Frankish medicine—as well as many other aspects of Frankish cul-

---

**13** Usama Ibn Munqidh, *An Arab-Syrian Gentleman and Warrior in the Period of the Crusades*, trans. Philip K. Hitti (New York: Columbia University Press, 2000), 162.

ture—this episode does highlight that physicians from both faiths did attend the same patients at the same time.

## Social Relations

However, among the most significant evidence is that which describes friendly social interactions, and indeed friendship, between followers of the two religions. Usama b. Munqidh reports the following:

> In the army of King Fulk [of Jerusalem], son of Fulk, was a Frankish reverend knight who had just arrived from their land in order to make the holy pilgrimage and then return home. He was of my intimate fellowship and kept such constant company with me that he began to call me "my brother." Between us were mutual bonds of amity and friendship. When he resolved to return by sea to his homeland, he said to me:

> My brother, I am leaving for my country and I want thee to send with me thy son (my [i.e., Usama's] son, who was then fourteen years old, was at that time in my company) to our company, where he can see the knights and learn wisdom and chivalry. When he returns, he will be like a wise man.

> Thus there fell upon my ears words which would never come out of the head of a sensible man; for even if my son were to be taken captive, his captivity could not bring him a worse misfortune than carrying him into the lands of the Franks. However, I said to the man:

> By thy life, this has exactly been my idea. But the only thing that prevented me from carrying it out was the fact that his grandmother, my mother, is so fond of him and did not this time let him come out with me until she exacted an oath from me to the effect that I would return him to her.

> Thereupon he asked, "Is thy mother still alive?" "Yes," I replied. "Well," said he, "disobey her not."[14]

This is a particularly telling passage. To the original audience, medieval Muslims, this story would have provoked both

---

14 Usama Ibn Munqidh, *An Arab-Syrian Gentleman and Warrior*, 161.

mirth and incomprehension, because the idea that a better education could be found in Europe rather than in the Middle East would have been a preposterous notion. Indeed, Usama deliberately included it in order to elicit such a response by highlighting the ludicrousness of the un-named Frank's suggestion. Yet, reading closely, it is also possible to view the interaction in a very different way. Four aspects stand out. First, that Usama was on such friendly terms with the Frankish knight that he "was of my intimate fellowship and kept such constant company with me that he began to call me 'my brother'." Second, there is no evidence of malice in his friend's suggestion that Usama's son go to Europe to be educated; rather, it seems to have been a sincere offer that was expected to improve the boy's life. Third, Usama did not want to offend his friend by ridiculing the idea to his face, and so offers an excuse that would prevent the boy from going without causing offence. Finally, the knight, taking at face value Usama's excuse, shows sensitivity to the situation and so tells Usama not to break his vow to the grandmother. Reading it this way, the passage therefore highlights a deep level of friendship and understanding between the Frank and the Muslim.

Further detailed evidence for such cordial relations is, like many other aspects, generally lacking. Nevertheless, some additional information regarding the kind of social relations that developed between the Franks and Muslims is implicit in a set of laws drawn up by the Frankish rulers in 1120. These laws, the Canons of the Council of Nablus, are focused on controlling social relations between Latin Christians and other groups, particularly Muslims. They include prohibitions on acts such as sex between a Muslim man and Christian woman, and between a Christian man and a Muslim slave. Attempts such as these to enact and enforce legislation on sexual relations between members of different religious communities was not new and had been seen since at least Roman times. Modern research into these law codes has suggested that they were almost exclusively drawn up not as proactive but rather as reactive measures. In other words, these legislative efforts were aimed at controlling social interactions that were already commonplace and perceived to be a significant problem, at least in the eyes of the elites. As such, it can be stated with a strong degree of certainty that Christians and Muslims did engage in sexual contacts of the type described above. This legal code thus not only acts as a witness to the judicial system in the crusader states but also to societal trends perceived to be problematic by the ruling elites.

Poems written by Muslims in praise of the beauty of the pale-skinned Frankish women are further witnesses to this. Many of these dwell on the beauty and the alluring nature of the Frankish women, whose fair skin and blonde hair had rarely been seen in the eastern Mediterranean before the Crusades. Even the extremely cantankerous and self-righteous Ibn Jubayr could not help but praise their beauty when passing through Frankish territory, although he is careful to qualify this with the statement: "We were thus given the chance of seeing this alluring sight, from the seducement of which God preserve us."[15] Like his assessment of the good treatment given to Muslim peasants by Frankish landlords, he sees these Frankish women's appearance merely as a trick, like the Sirens of Greek mythology, designed to lure good Muslim men to their destruction.

## Shared Religious Activity

In a famous episode, Usama b. Munqidh once more recalls an experience he had with the Franks, this time in Jerusalem:

> Whenever I visited Jerusalem I always entered the Aqsa mosque, beside which stood a small mosque which the Franks had converted into a church. When I used to enter the Aqsa mosque, which was occupied by the [Knights] Templars, who were my friends, the Templars would evacuate the little adjoining mosque so that I might pray in it. One day I entered this mosque, repeated the first formula [of the prayer], "Allah is great," and stood up in the act of pray-

---

**15** Ibn Jubayr, *The Travels of Ibn Jubayr*, 321.

ing, upon which one of the Franks rushed on me, got hold of me and turned my face eastwards saying "This is the way thou shouldest pray!" A group of Templars hastened to him, seized him and repelled him from me. I resumed my prayer. The same man, while the others were otherwise busy, rushed once more on me and turned my face eastward, saying "This is the way thou shouldest pray!" The Templars again came in to him and expelled him. They apologized to me, saying, "This is a stranger who has only recently arrived from the land of the Franks and he has never before seen anyone praying except eastward." Thereupon I said to myself, "I have had enough prayer." So I went out and have ever been surprised at the conduct of this devil of a man, at the change in the color of his face, his trembling and his sentiment at the sight of one praying towards the *qiblah* [i.e., Mecca].[16]

In addition to highlighting once again the existence of close friendship between himself and some of the Franks—in this case, the Templars, part of the backbone of the Franks' fighting forces—two other points are significant. First, although the unnamed man becomes quite agitated at Usama's praying to the south, there does not appear to be any malice in his attempts to persuade Usama. He seems instead to believe that he was making a genuine mistake. Second, and particularly significantly, this episode demonstrates that the Franks had allowed a mosque to remain in Jerusalem for Muslims to pray in. And this was not limited to Jerusalem alone, as Ibn Jubayr, for example, also records the existence of mosques in Frankish Tyre and in Acre.

Yet Usama's story of Jerusalem not only demonstrates the survival of Muslim places of worship under Frankish rule, it also highlights that some of those spaces were used by both religious groups. More evidence of this is provided by Ibn Jubayr:

To the east [of Acre] is the spring called Ayn Baqar...over it is a mosque of which there remains in its former state only the mihrab, to the east of which the Franks have built their own mihrab; and Muslim and infidel [i.e., Frank] assemble there, the one turning to his place of worship, the other to his. In the hands of the Christians its venerableness is maintained, and God has preserved in it a place of prayer for the Muslims.[17]

There are also examples of spaces that were regarded as primarily or even exclusively Christian, but which Muslims also frequented for religious reasons. These included the site of the Nativity in Bethlehem and the fields outside the town where the shepherds were; the tomb of Mary; the location of the wedding at Cana; and the icon of the Blessed Virgin of Our Lady at Saidnaya, among many others.[18]

Ordinary Muslims could even take part in Christian religious festivities, such as those of Palm Sunday and other events commemorating the Passion of Christ. This reached its zenith at the time of the descent of the Holy Fire, which spontaneously lit oil lamps in the Church of the Holy Sepulchre in Jerusalem on Easter Saturday each year, at which Muslims joined in this most Christian of events. Muslim participation in these Christian festivals is reported in both Christian sources and the writings of Muslims such as al-Turtushi (d. 1126), though with hostility on the part of the latter, who was especially averse to and so deplored such intercommunal festivities, and sought to prevent them from occurring.[19]

As well as this kind of interaction, Christian Franks and Muslims also travelled together on pilgrimage. Ibn Jubayr relates his journey from Acre, in the crusader state of Jerusalem, to Sicily, in 1184. He travelled on board a Genoese ship

---

**17** Ibn Jubayr, *The Travels of Ibn Jubayr*, 318–19.

**18** Andrew Jotischky, "Pilgrimage, Procession and Ritual Encounters between Christians and Muslims in the Crusader States," in *Cultural Encounters during the Crusades*, ed. Kurt V. Jensen, Kirsi Salonen, and Helle Vogt (Odense: University Press of Southern Denmark, 2013), 245–62.

**19** Alexander Mallett, "Two Writings of al-Turtushi as Evidence for Early Muslim Reactions to the Frankish Crusader Presence in the Levant," in *Weiner Zeitschrift fur die Kunde des Morgenlandes* 107 (2017): 143–78.

and provided a detailed account of the experience. Travelling with him were, he relates, more than two thousand Christian pilgrims on their way back to Europe. Throughout, he is careful to underline, the Muslims—by which he primarily means himself—secured lodging separate from the Christians, thereby keeping themselves ritually pure. However, his account also contains enough information about the customs and mores of the Franks onboard the ships to allow us to infer that there was significant interaction during the voyage. For example, he relates numerous Italian technical shipping terms that he must have learned on the voyage from the Christians; he provides a fairly detailed account of Frankish inheritance rules regarding those that die at sea (i.e., that the captain of the vessel inherits their possessions); and he shows fairly good knowledge of the geopolitical situation in the Christian world, such as the fact that the Franks were as hostile to their fellow-Christians, the Byzantines, as they were to the Muslims.

A final aspect is that people could help or comfort each other on matters of faith across the religious divide. Ibn Jubayr relates the kindness shown by local Christians towards the Muslim ascetics who lived around Mount Lebanon:

> It is strange how the Christians round Mount Lebanon, when they see any Muslim hermits, bring them food and treat them kindly, saying that these men are dedicated to Great and Glorious God and that they should therefore share with them.[20]

A particularly notable example of this is recorded in the work of the French notable John of Joinville who participated in the crusade of Louis IX of France to Egypt in the years around 1250. The crusade was ended by the defeat of Louis' forces at the Battle of Mansura in February that year, and Joinville was one of many taken prisoner by the Egyptian forces. He gives a lengthy and extremely vivid eyewitness account of the situation faced by the prisoners. Especially noteworthy is the kind treatment he says he received from various Mus-

---

**20** Ibn Jubayr, *The Travels of Ibn Jubayr*, 300.

lims. For example, on one day he was given some meat as food by one of the Muslims, which he ate. This horrified some of his fellow-Christians, who pointed out that, unbeknown to Joinville, it was a Friday, a day during which Latin Christians were not permitted to eat meat. A Muslim "admiral" asked why Joinville had become so upset and, when he was told the reason, comforted Joinville by saying "that God would not hold this against me since I had not done it knowingly."[21] On another occasion during his captivity, Joinville believed he was going to die as a result of an abscess in his throat, but a Muslim commander gave him some medicine which cured it and thus, he relates, saved his life.[22]

## Socio-Cultural Activities

Finally, there is significant evidence of various Franks partaking of specifically Muslim, or at least Middle Eastern, cultural activities. One of these was going to the bath-houses. As so often, a good—and amusing—example comes from Usama ibn Munqidh, who recounts the words of a bath-house owner named Salim:

> I once opened a bath in al-Ma'arrah in order to earn my living. To this bath there came a Frankish knight. The Franks disapprove of girding a cover around one's waist while in the bath. So this Frank stretched out his arm and pulled off my cover from my waist and threw it away. He looked and saw that I had recently shaved off my pubes. So he shouted, "Salim!" As I drew near him he stretched his hand over my pubes and said, "Salim, good! By the truth of my religion, do the same for me." Saying this, he lay on his back and I found that in that place the hair was like his beard. So I shaved it off. Then he passed his hand over the place and, finding it smooth, he said, "Salim, by the truth of my religion, do the

---

21 John of Joinville, *The Life of St. Louis*, trans. Caroline Smith, in *Joinville and Villehardouin, Chronicles of the Crusades* (London: Penguin, 2008), 227.

22 Joinville, *Life of St. Louis*, 226.

same to madame," referring to his wife. He then said to a servant of his, "Tell madame to come here." Accordingly the servant went and brought her and made her enter the bath. She also lay on her back. The knight repeated, "Do what thou hast done to me." So I shaved all that hair while her husband was sitting looking at me. At last he thanked me and handed me the pay for my service.[23]

As is the case in practically all of Usama's anecdotes, this was meant to evoke amusement and incredulity in a Muslim audience because of the ridiculousness of the Franks' behaviour, neatly encapsulated by the knight who has, to the Muslim audience, no sense of propriety. This is especially the case when he summons his wife, who should not have been allowed into the bath-house at the same time as the men, and then asks a complete stranger to shave her genitalia. To someone accustomed to the culture of the Middle East, such an act would be unimaginable. However, as before with the story of the knight who wanted to take Usama's son to Europe, a careful reading of this story reveals other aspects of inter-cultural exchange during this time, particularly the fact that the knight went to a Middle Eastern bath-house and engaged with Muslims when doing so was not an activity carried out in Europe.

Going further into acclimatizing to the Middle Eastern environ was a Frank who reportedly took on Muslim food and dietary laws. Usama ibn Munqidh relates that another Muslim told him:

We [the narrator and his friend] came to the house of a knight who belonged to the old category of knights who came with the early expeditions of the Franks. He had been by that time stricken off the register and exempted from service, and possessed in Antioch an estate on the income of which he lived. The knight presented an excellent table, with food extraordinarily clean and delicious. Seeing

---

**23** Usama Ibn Munqidh, *An Arab-Syrian Gentleman and Warrior*, 165–66.

me abstaining from food, he said, "Eat, be of good cheer! I never eat Frankish dishes, but I have Egyptian women cooks and never eat except their cooking. Besides, pork never enters my home." I ate, but guardedly, and after that we departed.[24]

As well as these examples of Frankish participation in Muslim socio-cultural events, Muslims are known to have attended those of the Franks. Again, it is Usama who recounts many of these, such as his presentation of the Frankish system of justice he witnessed:

They [the Franks] installed a huge cask and filled it with water. Across it they set a board of wood. They then bound the arms of the man [a Muslim] charged with the act [of killing Franks], tied a rope around his shoulders and dropped him into the cask, their idea being that in case he was innocent, he would sink in the water and they would lift him up with the rope and he might not die in the water; and in case he was guilty, he would not sink in the water. The man did his best to sink when they dropped him into the water, but he could not do it. So he had to submit to their sentence against him – may Allah's curse be upon them! They pierced his eyeballs with red-hot awls.[25]

Here, again, the Franks' inherent ridiculousness is pushed to the forefront. However, it does show once more that Muslims attended such Frankish events and suggests that this was not an unusual occurrence. Indeed, other examples of this are found in Usama's work, including his witnessing of a duel between two Frankish knights in Nablus, attending a Frankish feast, and bonding with the Franks over a shared passion for hunting.

A final example comes in the travel account of Ibn Jubayr. During his stay in Tyre in 1184 he witnessed a Frankish marriage ceremony, and describes the scene in some detail. The

---

**24** Usama Ibn Munqidh, *An Arab-Syrian Gentleman and Warrior*, 169–70.

**25** Usama Ibn Munqidh, *An Arab-Syrian Gentleman and Warrior*, 168–69.

bride, whose looks were the cause of his aforementioned comments regarding the attractiveness of Frankish women, moved through the town in a procession, wearing a beautiful dress and dripping with jewelry. On the side-lines, watching this spectacle, were not only members of the local Christian community but many Muslims as well—including Ibn Jubayr—who had chosen to witness, and thus participate in, this Frankish wedding procession.[26]

**26** Ibn Jubayr, *The Travels of Ibn Jubayr*, 320–21.

Chapter 6

# Religious Conversion

In his account of his journey through Frankish territory in the eastern Mediterranean in the early 1180s, the Spanish Muslim Ibn Jubayr relates a story he had been told of a Muslim convert to Christianity. This Muslim was originally from Buna, in modern Algeria, and:

> In one of his patron's caravans had come to [Frankish] Acre, where he had mixed with the Christians, and taken on much of their character. The devil increasingly seduced and incited him until he renounced the faith of Islam, turned unbeliever, and became a Christian.....He had been baptised and become unclean, and had put on the girdle of a monk, thereby hastening for himself the flames of hell, verifying the threats of torture, and exposing himself to a grievous account and a long-distant return (from hell).[1]

Ibn Jubayr's rather bigoted comments make little sense from the everyday perspective of the eastern Mediterranean in the crusading period, however, because such conversions were a regular occurrence in the twelfth and thirteenth centuries. They were so regular, in fact, that they elicit barely a comment from most of the other writers who mention them. Muslims could, and did, convert to Christianity, while Christians could, and did, convert to Islam. This chapter will briefly explore some examples of people who changed their religion

---

1 Ibn Jubayr, *The Travels of Ibn Jubayr*, 323.

and why they did so, highlighting that the Frankish presence in the Holy Land actually helped facilitate conversions in both directions and thereby permitted, in some ways, a larger degree of religious freedom than existed at other times in the region.

## Religious Conversion during the Crusading Period

The Latin chronicler of the First Crusade Albert of Aachen relates that, as early as August 1099, just a month after the capture of Jerusalem, the ruler of the city—Godfrey of Bouillon—had in his entourage a former Muslim who fought alongside the king at the Battle of Ascalon, in which the crusading army defeated a Muslim relief force from Egypt. Godfrey had persuaded the Muslim to convert to Christianity, and for years afterwards he remained a loyal servant to the rulers of Jerusalem. Albert's report is just one of dozens of instances of conversions by Muslims to Christianity that are mentioned in passing in the sources. For example, a little time after, the chronicler Fulcher of Chartres reports that King Baldwin I, the next ruler of Jerusalem, journeyed towards the Dead Sea region with some locals who had originally been Muslims but had converted to Christianity. In 1112, another convert to Christianity learned of a Muslim plot to attack Jerusalem, but warned the Christian authorities about it and so averted the threat. Finally, a throwaway line in a text relating the lives of pious Muslims from the Nablus region in the second half of the twelfth century relates that a Muslim from the area became a Christian. Clear examples such as these, and other instances that are merely hinted at—such as the presence of a certain Walter Muhammad, whose name demonstrates that he was a convert, in the government of the Kingdom of Jerusalem in the early twelfth century—underline that there were significant numbers of conversions.[2] Another factor that does so was the need for laws to govern how such converts

---

**2** For more details, see Mallett, *Popular Muslim Reactions*, 105–19.

were to be treated. For instance, a treaty signed between the Franks and the Mamluks in the 1280s contains a clause demonstrating that people from both sides were fleeing to the other's territory and there converting.

Religious conversion happened in all directions in the crusading period, and many Latin Christians converted to Islam. One particularly striking account of this can be found in an account of the Second Crusade (1147–49), entitled *De Profectione Ludovici in Orientem*, by the French writer Odo of Deuil. In this, following a crusader defeat outside Adalia, in Anatolia, that left practically the entire Frankish fighting force there dead, the Turks approached the survivors, almost all of whom were non-combatants and many of them sick. Rather than killing them as they had expected, the Turks saw their enfeebled state and took pity on them, giving them alms. In response to this, thousands of these Latin Christians, seeing that they were treated better by the Turks than by their fellow-Christians—specifically, the Greeks—joined the Turks and voluntarily converted to Islam.[3]

As well as conversions between Islam and Christianity, there are also a number of briefly recorded instances of conversions between Judaism and Christianity. At the very beginning of the crusading period, around 1102, for example, a Norman Christian from southern Italy—who seems to have been from the ranks of the nobility and who went on the First Crusade—converted to Judaism. Little is known of

---

**3** Odo of Deuil, *De Profectione Ludovici in Orientem*, trans. Virginia G. Berry (New York: Norton, 1948). Further evidence is provided by chronicles that detail mass conversions of Christians to Islam, such as those that occurred during the course of the Fifth Crusade, by a set of secular laws from the time of King Baldwin II of Jerusalem (r. 1118–1132) in which the legal status of Christians who become Muslims is dictated, and by various letters between churchmen regarding specific ecclesiastical legal positions, such as that of the still-Christian spouses of converts to Islam; see Benjamin Z. Kedar, "Multidirectional Conversion in the Frankish Levant," in *Varieties of Religious Conversion in the Middle Ages*, ed. James Muldoon (Gainesville: University Press of Florida, 1997), 190–208.

him except that he took the name Obadayah upon entering his new faith, that he is mentioned several times in letters found in the trove of documents from Cairo known as the Geniza collection, and that he left a brief account of his later life in Baghdad, where he seems to have settled. More evidence is provided by the famous Jewish doctor Maimonides, who lived in Egypt in the latter half of the twelfth century and wrote of several Christians who became Jews. Conversions could also happen in the other direction, and there are several examples of these in the sources. In the immediate aftermath of the Frankish capture of Jerusalem in 1099, for example, a number of Jews converted to Christianity. Later in the thirteenth century, Jewish converts to Christianity are referred to in papal letters—for example, those written by Pope Urban IV in 1264—in which poor Jews are reported to have left Muslim for Christian territory in an attempt to escape poverty. Another letter, from 1198, discusses in practical terms the legal position of these converted Jews. Conversions between Judaism and Christianity do, however, seem to have been much less frequent than those between Islam and Christianity, and there are significantly fewer references to it in the sources, no doubt mainly because there were comparatively small numbers of Jews.

## Why People Converted

In modern times, conversion between religions is often seen as being an individual act carried out for reasons of faith alone, and there is some limited evidence for such conversions during the crusading period. Ibn Jubayr's aforementioned passage contains perhaps the clearest example of this, as the convert's devotion to his new religion was so strong that he not only converted but also became a monk. The text recalling the pious Muslims of Nablus, also mentioned above, makes passing reference to a Muslim "who entered a church and became a Christian." These acts, which may be termed "true conversions," are fairly rare in the sources, although, as Kedar has pointed out, they "are not presented as exceptional."[4] In other words, it is likely that they happened fairly often but that there was little desire, on either side, to record them.

Most examples of conversions for reasons of belief seem to have been individuals who had originally been forced to convert to one or the other religion, and then were able at some point to return to their original faith. For example, a Frankish slave named Raul, who served the father of Usama ibn Munqidh, had converted to Islam and was given a Muslim wife. Some years after his conversion, however, he fled with his wife and children back to Frankish territory where they all converted to Christianity. Another example comes from the time of a treaty agreed between Damascus and Jerusalem in 1136. According to this agreement, anyone living in Damascus who had originally been a Christian but then was captured and forced to convert to Islam was allowed to leave the city for Frankish lands if they wanted to return to their former faith. The vast majority of those given that opportunity took it.

Yet conversion as the result of religious conviction was only one among a number of reasons for which people seem to have changed their faith, and certainly one of the rarest. There were numerous other reasons as well, none of which were specific to just one religion. These include people who converted in order to save their own lives, of which there are dozens of examples recorded in the sources. To cite just one, from the time of the Third Crusade, the army of the Kingdom of Jerusalem had been supplemented by arrivals from Europe, and had encircled and was besieging the Muslim-held port-city of Acre. However, they themselves were, in turn, surrounded by Saladin's forces, trapped with the walls of the city behind them and a Muslim army in front of them. As a result, they quickly ran low on food and were ravaged by disease, thereby leading to many of the Franks abandoning the siege, crossing over to Saladin's forces, and converting to Islam simply just to get something to eat.

---

4 Kedar, "Multidirectional Conversion in the Frankish Levant," 191.

Another comes from the time of the Crusade of Louis IX of France to Egypt, in the years around 1250. During this, the French army was defeated at Mansura, on the road from the Mediterranean coast to Cairo. Those who were not killed in the battle were captured, including the eyewitness, John of Joinville. In his account, he describes how the Muslims succeeded in their attempts to force some of the captured Franks, at least, to convert to Islam:

> Many of the knights and other people were kept inside a courtyard enclosed by mud walls. The custom of our enemies was to take them from this enclosure, one by one, and ask them: "Are you willing to abjure your faith?" Those who refused to abjure were set on one side, and their heads were cut off; those who consented were kept the other side.[5]

This stark choice, between conversion and death, was experienced many times by both Christians and Muslims during the crusading period. The great Arab chronicler of the thirteenth century, Ibn al-Athir, reports that four hundred Muslims from the town of Buza'a, in northern Syria, converted to Christianity in 1137–38, while those who did not were killed.[6] In one account of the First Crusade, a group of Muslim peasants was given the choice of death or conversion by some crusaders, as were the Muslims of Damietta when the city was captured by the Fifth Crusade in 1219.

However, such forced conversions may also have been less than sincere. For instance, the abovementioned Raul and the Christians from Damascus were evidently eager to return to their previous faith as soon as they could once they were given the opportunity. As a result, many contemporary observers were deeply skeptical about conversions made under duress. John of Joinville, for example, notes rather caustically:

> The [Muslim] admiral had all my sailors brought before me, and he told me that they had renounced their faith. I said

---

**5** Joinville, *Life of St. Louis*, 228.

**6** Ibn al-Athir, *Chronicle of Ibn al-Athir*, 1:340.

that he should not have any confidence in them for just as swiftly as they had abandoned us so would they abandon the Saracens [Muslims], if they saw a time or place to do so. And the admiral replied that he agreed with me, for Saladin said that one never saw a bad Christian become a good Saracen, nor a bad Saracen become a good Christian.[7]

Another reason for converting was in order to profit in some way materially. This is evident particularly often in the thirteenth century, in cases of Muslim slaves of Christians who converted to Christianity, or at least claimed to have done so. As was the case all over the medieval world, these slaves were predominantly caught during cross-border raiding, after which they were either kept by one of the raiding parties or sold. The main reason they converted was that the Latin Church had declared that, when a Muslim became a Christian, they should be freed, as part of a broader effort to encourage conversion. There are dozens of pieces of evidence for such conversions, both direct and indirect. In particular, papal letters and the writings of churchmen such as James of Vitry demonstrate that huge numbers of Muslim slaves were converting for this very reason. Indeed, the resulting number of Muslim slaves changing their religion within the crusader states was so large that specific pieces of legislation about them had to be drawn up from time to time. For example, there were so many Muslim converts in the Frankish capital of Acre in the 1260s that Pope Urban IV felt obliged to dictate the financial conditions under which they were to be supported.[8]

However, a very significant percentage of these conversions were actually faked, since many of these "converts" fled to Muslim land almost immediately after they had been freed by their Christian masters, where they immediately declared themselves to be Muslims once more. This became such a problem for the Latin Church that the legal status of

---

**7** Joinville, *Life of St. Louis*, 227.

**8** Benjamin Z. Kedar, *Crusade and Mission. European Approaches towards the Muslims* (Princeton: Princeton University Press, 1984), 152.

slaves who had converted was changed: they no longer had the right to be freed automatically after conversion. The particularly pious King Louis IX of France, however, rather cleverly managed to get around this. During his time in the Holy Land around 1250, he bought and then freed a large number of Muslim slaves after they had converted, but sent them on to live in France, where it would have been all but impossible for them to escape back to Muslim territory and thereby return to Islam.

Finally, some people seem to have converted in order to profit much more fully in material terms. For example, an Englishman named Robert of St. Albans, who joined Saladin in 1185, became a significant figure in the Muslim world after converting because that society was much more amenable to social mobility. It would remain so right into the early-modern period, and was the main reason so many Europeans moved to Muslim lands and converted to Islam over the centuries.

Religious conversions in the crusading period were almost never purely a religious exercise. They never could be, when religion, politics, "nationality," language, and identity were as tightly interwoven as they were in medieval times. Most conversions were an exercise in politics, and particularly an exercise in people attempting to gain some kind of an advantage for themselves. Whether that was escaping death, being freed from slavery, or gaining material or political advantage, conversions were primarily an act of the self.

## Who Converted

The sources suggest that the vast majority of converts were from the lower reaches of society. The notables, on the other hand, generally did not. There are certain identifiable reasons for this. The lower ranks of society certainly had cause to convert, for reasons noted above: slaves of Christian masters converted to gain their freedom; people who saw a material advantage; and those who did so in order to avoid being executed.

The most elevated members of both societies, on the other hand, did not have the material or financial problems that drove many of their co-religionists to convert. Principally, though, it was the result of the specific circumstances around one of the most regular types of conversion: forced conversions after a battle had been lost. Unlike the members of the lower classes, the nobles were seen as a valuable asset because they could ransom themselves for particularly high sums. So, instead of being given the choice of death or conversion, they were kept languishing in prison, sometimes for many years, until their co-religionists paid for them to be released. For example, Prince Reynald of Châtillon, who was a particular thorn in Saladin's side in the 1180s, had been released from captivity in Aleppo in 1176 after spending around sixteen years in the city's dungeon following the handover of the astronomical sum of 120,000 dinars. As such, there are only occasional mentions of high-ranking members of society converting. The headman of the northern Syrian town of Saruj did so sometime before 1109; the chief Muslim judge of Buza'a, also in northern Syria, did so in 1137, as did the son of the sultan of Konya (in modern Turkey). On the Christian side, a handful converted to Islam, such as the aforementioned Robert of St. Albans. However, these were very much the exception. Almost exclusively, the converts were from the lower levels of society.[9]

## Temporal Trends of Conversion

While the various examples given above have sketched just a few instances of religious conversion during the crusading period, the sources contain many more. They start with the first major victory by the crusaders, their capture of the city of Antioch in 1098, where several sources report conversions by some of the Muslims there—in one case, as many as a thousand. They go on to the final decade, as surviving treaties between the Franks and Muslims highlight that significant numbers, from both sides, were converting. However, at first glance the sources do not suggest that there was a steady stream of converts across the period. Rather, recorded instances

---

**9** Mallett, *Popular Muslim Reactions*, 109–10.

of either conversion or issues related to it see a significant increase in the thirteenth century compared to the twelfth.

This would seem to indicate that there was a concomitant increase in the number of conversions between the two periods. However, this cannot be taken for granted, for two main reasons. First, on the European side, during the twelfth century there had been a minority of Christians who had had reservations regarding the permissibility of fighting in order to spread the faith. During much of this period, however, such qualms had been tempered by the fact that Christian successes in their adventures meant that it seemed like God had blessed their military expedition against the Muslims with victory. This changed following the setbacks the Franks had begun to suffer, especially following the loss of Jerusalem and almost all the crusader states to Saladin in 1187. At this point, the number of people inside the Latin Church who were opposed to fighting the Muslims and in favour of trying to convert them began to grow because, it seemed, God did not support—or no longer supported—the crusading enterprise. This can be seen clearly in the writings and actions of a number of churchmen, usually from the mendicant orders of monks whose main role was to preach Christianity.

St. Francis of Assisi, as mentioned above, provides one of the best examples of this when he attempted to convert the Egyptian sultan to Christianity through preaching. In this he was, unsurprisingly, unsuccessful, but his efforts struck a chord in Europe and were recounted for centuries after. This attempt was particularly striking because it was so firmly against the grain of what else was happening. Christians from the crusader camp were defecting to the Muslim side and converting in such numbers at the time that it was originally believed that St. Francis was also crossing into the camp to do so.[10]

The second reason is the state of the sources. Those recounting the first century or so of the crusading period, before Saladin's campaigns, are fairly dry and terse chron-

---

**10**  Kedar, "Multidirectional Conversion in the Frankish Levant," 194.

icles, focusing almost exclusively on battles and high-level politicking. Thus, low-level acts of conversion are ignored. With Saladin's time, not only do the chronicles become much more detailed, but other genres start to be written; these include documents, such as the treaties mentioned above; life stories, such as that of Usama ibn Munqidh; travel narratives, such as that of Ibn Jubayr; and biography, such as those by Baha al-Din Ibn Shaddad and John of Joinville. With these much more detailed, sometimes day-by-day reports of events, there is much more opportunity for such conversions to be seen in the sources.

## Conclusion: The Provision of Religious Freedom

Religious freedom may not be the most obvious consequence of the Crusades, certainly not from a popular perspective. Yet the Frankish presence did allow an almost unprecedented level of freedom to convert. For Muslims who wanted to convert to Christianity, the existence of the crusader states provided a rare opportunity to do so, as they mitigated the obvious dangers, most notably the Islamic legal injunction to kill apostates, something that was widely practised in the medieval Middle East, as many writers, both Christian and Muslim, attest. Not only was this the case in militantly Sunni Muslim societies such as the Mamluk one (r. 1250–1517), but also in comparatively tolerant ones, such as that of the Ayyubids (1193–1250). To give just one example, around the year 1210 a Christian in Egypt named John of Phanijoit converted to Islam and then reconverted to his former faith, which resulted in his execution upon the orders of the Ayyubid sultan al-Kamil. The presence of the Frankish states in Syria and Palestine allowed converts to Christianity, at least, a possible means of escape from this situation that had not previously existed. For the Latin Christians, too, the existence of the crusader states allowed for a greater measure of religious freedom. Anyone born and raised in Latin Europe would have had little opportunity to encounter or engage with Islam unless they lived in the Iberian Peninsula. The existence of the crusader states changed that. Large numbers of Latin Christians travelled to the Holy Land where they could encounter Islam for the first time—not always peaceably, of course—and those who wished to convert were able to do so, after which they could move to nearby Muslim lands to see out the rest of their days.

# Concluding Remarks

The Crusades have traditionally been viewed through the lenses of military conflict and the activities—military, religious, or political—of the elite men of action (they were almost always, though not exclusively, men) on both sides. This should be seen as a consequence of the fact that the sources on which we rely for information were almost exclusively written by and, especially, for members of the same elite groups. Furthermore, the circumstances in which they were composed means that conflict, rather than co-operation, is primarily celebrated, and even comparatively tolerant writers such as Ibn Wasil felt the need to clearly justify why his masters were failing to attack the Franks.

However, these attitudes cannot be said to have been shared by the remainder of society, as indeed there is evidence to suggest that those outside the urban and educated elites held very different priorities. The nature of the sources means it is comparatively difficult to see them, but they are there, whether in throwaway remarks in a chronicle or in the various comments of the two writers who provide us with the clearest evidence of day-to-day life in the eastern Mediterranean during this time, Usama ibn Munqidh and Ibn Jubayr. The evidence thus suggests that, alongside the set-piece conflict that dominates the narrative of the crusading period, there was a parallel temporality in which Latin Christians and Muslims lived and worked alongside each other. This meant that, in terms of diplomacy, the exchange of scientific and religious knowledge, everyday life, and religious conversion, there were significant levels of interaction, communication, and relationship building between Latin Christians and Muslims, as well as other groups such as Jews. These interactions, in turn, helped to create conditions for the swift exchange of further mutual knowledge. Accordingly, away from the bombastic propaganda of much of the source material, everyday life in and around the crusader states was as tolerant and mutually co-operative as anywhere else in the medieval world, and perhaps predominantly more so.

# Further Reading

Abulafia, David. "Trade and Crusade, 1050–1250." In *Cross-Cultural Convergences in the Crusader Period: Essays Presented to Aryeh Grabois on his Sixty-Fifth Birthday*, edited by Michael Goodich, Sophia Menache, and Sylvia Schein, 1–20. New York: Lang, 1995.

> Excellent overview of trade in the period and how it led to significant contacts between members of the two communities.

Burnett, Charles. *Arabic into Latin in the Middle Ages: The Translators and their Intellectual and Social Contexts*. Variorum Collected Studies Series. Farnham: Ashgate, 2009.

> A collection of articles about the movement of texts and ideas from the Islamic world to Europe in the medieval period, written by a leading expert on the subject.

Christie, Niall. *Muslims and Crusaders: Christianity's Wars in the Middle East, 1095–1382, from the Islamic Sources*. Second Edition. London: Routledge, 2020.

> An excellent political history of the period from the Muslim perspective, containing an extremely useful appendix of translated Arabic sources.

Cobb, Paul M. *The Race for Paradise: An Islamic History of the Crusades*. Oxford: Oxford University Press, 2014.

> Another excellent overview of the history of the Crusades from the Muslim standpoint. Unlike Christie's text, this also includes events in Sicily and Iberia in the twelfth and thirteenth centuries.

*Christian Muslim Relations: A Bibliographical History.* Volumes 3 and 4. Edited by David Thomas and Alex Mallett. Leiden: Brill, 2011–2012.

> Contains encyclopaedia-style entries on all the primary sources in which Christians wrote about or against Islam and Muslims about or against Christianity. As such, virtually all texts relevant to the crusading period are included. These volumes cover the period 1050–1350.

Hillenbrand, Carole. *The Crusades: Islamic Perspectives.* Edinburgh: Edinburgh University Press, 1999.

> The essential text for Muslim perceptions of and relations with the Franks.

Holt, P. M. *The Age of the Crusades.* London: Longman, 1986.

> Rather old but still eminently useful account of the history of the eastern Mediterranean in the later medieval period.

Housley, Norman. *Contesting the Crusades.* Oxford: Blackwell, 2006.

> This is a brilliant and very accessible introduction to the various competing modern interpretations of aspects of the crusading movement, although it is focused almost wholly on the Latin Christian perspective.

Humphreys, R. Stephen. *From Saladin to the Mongols.* Albany: State University of New York Press, 1977.

> Detailed study of the city of Damascus under Ayyubid rule.

Ibn Jubayr. *The Travels of Ibn Jubayr.* Translated by R. J. C. Broadhurst. London: Cape, 1952.

> Despite his sanctimonious attitude, Ibn Jubayr provides some of the best evidence for Christian–Muslim relations from the whole crusading period, through an account of his journey through the Holy Land in 1184.

Jacoby, David. "Aspects of Everyday Life in Frankish Acre." In *Crusades* 4 (2005): 73–105.

> An in-depth study of everyday life in what was the Frankish capital for a hundred years.

John of Joinville. *The Life of St. Louis.* Translated by Caroline Smith. London: Penguin, 2008.

> Extremely vivid and entertaining account of the Seventh Crusade written by an eyewitness participant.

Jotischky, Andrew. "Pilgrimage, Procession and Ritual Encounters between Christians and Muslims in the Crusader States." In *Cultural Encounters during the Crusades*, edited by Kurt Villads Jensen, Kirsi Salonen, and Helle Vogt, 245–62. Odense: University Press of Southern Denmark, 2013.

A useful exploration of the use of religious sites by followers of both religions during the crusading period.

Kedar, B. Z. *Crusade and Mission: European Approaches towards the Muslims*. Princeton: Princeton University Press, 1984.

A detailed study of the interplay between the crusading movement in the Middle East and attempts to convert Muslims to Christianity.

Kedar, B. Z. *Franks, Muslims and Oriental Christians in the Latin Levant*. Variorum Collected Studies Series. Aldershot: Ashgate, 2006.

This is a collection of scholarly articles by an academic whose primary focus has been interactions between Christians and Muslims in the crusading period.

Köhler, Michael A. *Alliances and Treaties between Frankish and Muslim Rulers in the Middle East*. Translated by P. M. Holt; revised by Konrad Hirschler. Leiden: Brill, 2013.

Extremely well researched and rather dense monograph study of diplomatic relations between Franks and Muslims in the crusading period, though it unfortunately focuses almost exclusively on the first hundred years and generally ignores the last century of encounters.

König, Daniel. *Arabic–Islamic Views of the Latin West*. Oxford: Oxford University Press, 2015.

Excellent study of the shifting ways in which Muslims viewed Latin Europe over the course of the medieval period, and particularly as a result of the Crusades.

Mallett, Alex. *Popular Muslim Reactions to the Franks in the Levant, 1097–1291*. Farnham: Ashgate, 2014.

Examines the under-researched area of how ordinary Muslims, rather than the political or religious elites, responded to the arrival and presence of the Franks in the Middle East.

*Medieval Muslim Historians and the Franks in the Levant*. Edited by Alex Mallett. Leiden: Brill, 2014.

Provides detailed introductory studies to seven of the main Muslim historians and their writings related to the crusading period. Another volume on the same subject is currently in preparation, expected to be published in 2023.

Mitchell, Piers. *Medicine in the Crusades: Warfare, Wounds, and the Medieval Surgeon*. Cambridge: Cambridge University Press, 2004.

> Introduction to many aspects of medical knowledge and practice in the crusader states.

Morton, Nicholas. *Encountering Islam on the First Crusade*. Cambridge: Cambridge University Press, 2016.

> Detailed study of Latin Christian views of Muslims at the very beginning of the crusading period.

Phillips, Jonathan P. *Holy Warriors: A Modern History of the Crusades*. London: The Bodley Head, 2009.

> Provides an exceptional, scholarly yet accessible overview of the Crusades and crusading ideology from the eleventh right up to the twentieth century.

Riley-Smith, Jonathan, and Louise Riley-Smith. *The Crusades: Idea and Reality, 1095–1274*. London: Arnold, 1981.

> A good collection of translated European-language primary source material related to the Crusades, exploring a variety of themes.

Riley-Smith, Jonathan. *What Were the Crusades?* Basingstoke: Palgrave Macmillan, 2009.

> One of the best introductory guides to the Crusades from the doyen of crusade studies in the late twentieth and early twenty-first century.

Rubin, Jonathan. *Learning in a Crusader City: Intellectual Activity and Intercultural Exchanges in Acre, 1191–1291*. Cambridge: Cambridge University Press, 2018.

> Overview of intercultural exchange in the Frankish capital during the thirteenth century.

Sidelko, Paul. "Muslim Taxation under Crusader Rule." In *Tolerance and Intolerance: Social Conflict in the Age of the Crusades*, edited by Michael Gervers and James M. Powell, 65–74. Syracuse: Syracuse University Press, 2001.

> Provides a detailed assessment of the tax system for Muslims living under Frankish rule in the crusader states.

Tolan, John. *Saracens: Islam in the Medieval European Imagination*. New York: Columbia University Press, 2002.

> An introduction to some of the main texts in which Latin European writers describe Islam.

Usama b. Munqidh. *The Book of Contemplation: Islam and the Crusades*. Translated by Paul M. Cobb. London: Penguin, 2008.

Excellent translation of probably the most detailed source on everyday interactions between Muslims and Christians in the crusading period. However, it should be read with caution as regards factual accuracy, since the truth comes a distant second to entertaining stories.